Richard Hurd

Moral and Political Dialogues

With Letters on Chivalry and Romance. Fifth Edition, Vol. II

Richard Hurd

Moral and Political Dialogues
With Letters on Chivalry and Romance. Fifth Edition, Vol. II

ISBN/EAN: 9783744675338

Printed in Europe, USA, Canada, Australia, Japan

Cover: Foto ©Thomas Meinert / pixelio.de

More available books at **www.hansebooks.com**

MORAL AND POLITICAL DIALOGUES;

WITH

LETTERS ON CHIVALRY AND ROMANCE:

BY

THE REVEREND DOCTOR HURD.

THE FIFTH EDITION.

VOLUME THE SECOND.

LONDON:
PRINTED FOR T. CADELL IN THE STRAND.
M DCC LXXVI.

CONTENTS.

VOL. II.

DIALOGUE IV.

On the Age of Q. ELIZABETH.
MR. DIGBY. DR. ARBUTHNOT, MR. ADDISON.

DIALOGUES V, VI.

On the Constitution of the English Government.
SIR J. MAYNARD, MR. SOMERS, BP. BURNET.

DIALOGUE IV.

On the Age of Queen ELIZABETH.

MR. DIGBY, DR. ARBUTHNOT, MR. ADDISON.

BUT do you confider, faid Mr. ADDISON, as they defcended into the valley, what an invidious tafk you are going to impofe upon me? One cannot call in queftion a common opinion in any indifferent matter, without the appearance of fome degree of perverfenefs. But to do it in a cafe of this importance, where the greateft authorities ftand in the way, and the glory of one of our princes is concerned, will, I doubt, be liable to the imputation of fomething worfe than fingularity. For, befides that you will be apt to upbraid me, in the words of the poet,

Nullum

Nullum memorabile nomen
Fœmineâ in pœnâ eſt, nec habet victoria
laudem,

ſuch a liberty of cenſure is uſually taken for an argument, not of diſcourteſy or preſumption only, but of ill-nature. At beſt, the attempt to arraign the virtues and government of ELIZABETH, will appear but like the idleneſs of the old ſophiſts, who, you know, were never ſo well pleaſed as when they were controverting ſome acknowledged fact, or aſſaulting ſome eſtabliſhed character.

THAT cenſure might be juſt enough, Dr. ARBUTHNOT ſaid, of the old ſophiſts, who had nothing in view but the credit of their own ſkill in the arts of diſputation. But in this friendly debate, which means nothing more than private amuſement, I ſee no colour for ſuch apprehenſions.

BUT what ſhall we ſay, interpoſed Mr. ADDISON, to another difficulty? The ſubject

subject is very large; and it seems no easy matter to reduce it into any distinct order. Besides, my business is not so much to advance any thing of my own, as to object to what others have advanced concerning the fame and virtues of ELIZABETH. And to this end, I must desire to know the particulars on which you are disposed to lay the greatest stress, and indeed to have some plan of the subject delivered in to me, which may serve, as it were, for the ground-work of the whole conversation.

I MUST not presume, said Dr. ARBUTHNOT, to prescribe the order in which your attack on the great queen shall be conducted. The subject, indeed, is large. But this common route of history is well known to all of us. To that, then, you may well enough refer, without being at the trouble, before you go to work, of laying foundations. Or, if you will needs have a basis to build upon,

upon, what if I just run over the several circumstances which I conceive to make most for the credit of that reign? A sketch of this sort, I suppose, will answer all the ends of the plan, you seem to require of me.

Mr. ADDISON agreed to this proposal; which he thought would be of use to shorten the debate, or at least to render the progress of it more clear and intelligible.

In few words then, resumed Dr. ARBUTHNOT, the reasons, that have principally determined me to an admiration of the government and character of queen ELIZABETH, are such as these: " That she came to the crown with all possible disadvantages; which yet, by the prudence and vigour of her counsels, she entirely overcame: that she triumphed over the greatest foreign and domestic dangers: that she humbled the most formidable

midable power in *Europe* by her arms; and compofed, or checked at leaft, by the firmnefs of her adminiftration, TWO, the moft implacable and firey factions at home: that fhe kept down the rebellious fpirit of *Ireland*, and eluded the conftant intrigues of her reftlefs neighbours, the *Scots*: that fhe fixed our religious eftablifhment on folid grounds, and countenanced, or rather conducted, the Proteftant caufe abroad: that fhe made her civil authority refpected by her fubjects; and raifed the military glory of the nation, both by fea and land, to the greateft height: that fhe employed the ableft fervants, and enacted the wifeft laws: by all which means it came to pafs that fhe lived in a conftant good underftanding with her parliaments, was idolized by her people, and admired and envied by all the reft of the world."

ALAS, faid Mr. ADDISON, I fhall never be able to follow you through all the particulars

particulars of this encomium: and, to say the truth, it would be to little purpose; since the wisdom of her policy, in all these instances of her government, can only be estimated from a careful perusal of the histories of that time; too numerous and contradictory to be compared and adjusted in this conversation. All I can do, continued he, after taking a moment or two to recollect himself, is to abate the force of this panegyric by some general observations of the CIRCUMSTANCES and GENIUS of that time; and then to consider the personal QUALITIES of the queen, which are thought to reflect so great a lustre on her government.

As you please, DR. ARBUTHNOT replied. We shall hardly lose ourselves in this beaten field of history. And, besides, as your undertaking is so adventurous, it is but reasonable you should have the choice of your own method.

You

You are in the common opinion, I perceive, refumed Mr. ADDISON, that ELIZABETH's government was attended with all poffible difadvantages. On the contrary, it appears to me that the fecurity and even fplendour of her reign is chiefly to be accounted for from the fortunate CIRCUMSTANCES of her fituation.

OF thefe the FIRST, that demands our notice, is the great affair of religion.

THE principles of PROTESTANTISM had now for many years been working among the people. They had grown to that head in the fhort reign of EDWARD VI, that the bloody feverities of his fucceffor ferved only to exafperate the zeal, with which thefe principles had been embraced and promoted. ELIZABETH, coming to the crown at this juncture, was determined, as well by intereft as inclination, to take the fide of the new religion. I say by *interest*, as well as inclination. And, I think, I have reason for the assertion. For though the persons in power, and the clergy throughout the kingdom, were generally professed papists; yet they were most of them such as had conformed in king EDWARD's days, and were not therefore much to be feared for any tie, their *profession* could really have on their consciences. Whereas, on the other hand, it was easy to see, from many symptoms, that the general bent of the nation was towards Protestantism; and that, too, followed with a spirit, which must in the end prevail over all opposition. Under these circumstances, then, it was natural for the queen, if she had not been otherwise led by her principles, and the interest of her title, to favour the Reformation.

THE truth is, she came into it herself so heartily, and provided so effectually for

for its eſtabliſhment, that we are not to wonder ſhe became the idol of the Reformed, at the ſame time that the papal power through all *Europe* was confederated againſt her. The enthuſiaſm of her Proteſtant ſubjects was prodigious. It was raiſed by other conſiderations: but confirmed in all orders of the ſtate by the eaſe they felt in their deliverance from the tyranny of the church; and in the great eſpecially, by the ſweets they taſted in their enjoyment of the church-revenues. It was, in ſhort, one of thoſe extraordinary conjunctures, in which the public danger becomes the public ſecurity; when religion and policy, conſcience and intereſt, unite their powers to ſupport the authority of the prince, and to give fidelity, vigour, and activity, to the obedience of the ſubject.

AND thus it was, continued he, that ſo warm and unconquerable a zeal appeared in defence of the queen againſt all

all attempts of her enemies. Her people were so thoroughly Protestant, as to think no expence of her government too great, provided they could but be secured from relapsing into Popery. And her parliaments were disposed to wave all disputes about the stretch of her prerogative, from a sense of their own and the common danger.

IN magnifying this advantage of the zeal and union of ELIZABETH's good subjects, you forgot, said Dr. ARBUTHNOT, that two restless and inveterate factions were contending, all her life-time, within her own kingdom.

I AM so far from forgetting that circumstance, returned Mr. ADDISON, that I esteem it ANOTHER of the great advantages of her situation.

THE contrary tendencies of those factions in some respects defeated each other.

other. But the principal use of them was, that, by means of their practices, some domestic plot, or foreign alarm, was always at hand, to quicken the zeal and inflame the loyalty of her people. But to be a little more particular about the factions of her reign.

The Papist was, in truth, the only one she had reason to be alarmed at. The Puritan had but just begun to shew himself, though indeed with that ferocity of air and feature, which signified clearly enough what spirit he was of, and what, in good time, he was likely to come to. Yet even he was kept in tolerable humour, by a certain commodious policy of the queen; which was, so to divide her regards betwixt the Church and the Puritans, as made it the interest of both to keep well with her. 'Tis true, these last felt the weight of her resentment sometimes, when they ventured too sawcily to oppose themselves to the
establishment.

establishment. But this was rarely, and by halves: and, when checked with the most rigour, they had the satisfaction to see their patrons continue in the highest places at court, and, what is more, in the highest degree of personal favour.

AND what doth all this shew, interrupted Dr. ARBUTHNOT, but that she managed so well as to disarm a furious faction, or rather make it serve against the bent of its nature, to the wise ends of her government?

As to any wise ends of government, I see none, replied Mr. ADDISON, deserving to be so called, that were answered by her uncertain conduct towards the Puritans. For she neither restrained them with that severity, which might perhaps have prevented their growth, at first; nor shewed them that entire indulgence, which might have disabled their fury afterwards. It is true, this
temporizing

temporizing conduct was well enough adapted to prevent disturbances in her own time. But large materials were laid in for that terrible combustion, which was soon to break forth under one of her successors.

AND so, instead of imputing the disasters that followed, said Dr. ARBUTHNOT, to the ill-government of the STUARTS, you are willing to lay the whole guilt of them on this last and greatest of the TUDORS. This is a new way of defending that royal house; and, methinks, they owe you no small acknowledgments for it. I confess, it never occurred to me to make that apology for them.

THOUGH I would not undertake, said Mr. ADDISON, to make their apology from this, or any other, circumstance; I do indeed believe that part of the difficulties the house of STUART had to encounter, were brought upon them by
this

this wretched policy of their predeceſſor: But, waving this conſideration, I deſire you will take notice of what I chiefly inſiſt upon, "That the eaſe and ſecurity of ELIZABETH's adminiſtration was even favoured by the turbulent practices and claſhing views of her domeſtic factions." The PURITAN was an inſtrument, in her hands, of controuling the church, and of balancing the power of her miniſters: beſides that this ſort of people were, of all others, the moſt inveterate againſt the common enemy. And for the PAPISTS themſelves (not to inſiſt that, of courſe, they would be ſtrictly watched, and that they were not, perhaps, ſo conſiderable as to create any immediate danger [a]), the general abhorrence both of their

[a] This will be admitted, if a calculation ſaid to have been made by themſelves of their number at that time may be relied on—"They make reaſoning (ſaith Sir EDWIN SANDYS in his *Speculum Europæ*, written in 1699) forty hundred ſure catholics in *England*, with four hundred *Engliſh Roman* prieſts to maintain that militia," p. 157.

principles

principles and designs had the greatest effect in uniting more closely, and cementing, as it were, the affections of the rest of her subjects. So that, whether within or without, the common danger, as 1 expressed it, was the common safety.

STILL, said Dr. ARBUTHNOT, I must think this a very extraordinary conclusion. I have no idea of the security of the great queen, surrounded, as she was, by her domestic and foreign enemies.

HER foreign enemies, returned Mr. ADDISON, were less formidable than they appear at first view. And I even make the condition of the neighbouring powers on the continent, in her time, a THIRD instance of the signal advantages of her situation.

IT is true, if a perfect union had subsisted between the Catholic princes, the papal thunders would have carried terror with them. But, as it was, they were powerless and ineffectual. The civil wars of *France*, and its constant jealousy of *Spain*, left the queen but little to apprehend from that quarter. The *Spanish* empire, indeed, was vast, and under the direction of a bigoted vindictive prince. But the administration was odious and corrupt in every part. So that wise men saw there was more of bulk than of force in that unwieldy monarchy. And the successful struggles of a handful of its subjects, inflamed by the love of liberty, and made furious by oppression, proclaimed its weakness to all the world.

It may be true, interrupted Dr. ARBUTHNOT, that the queen had less to fear from the princes on the continent, than is sometimes represented. But you forget, in this survey of the public dangers, the distractions of IRELAND, and the restless intrigues of her near neighbours, the SCOTS: both of them assisted

by

by *Spain*; and these last under the peculiar influence and direction of the GUISES.

You shall have my opinion, returned Mr. ADDISON, in few words.

FOR the IRISH distractions, it was not the queen's intention, or certainly it was not her fortune, to compose them: I mean, during the greatest part of her reign; for we are now speaking of the general tenor of her policy. Towards the close of it, indeed, she made some vigorous attempts to break the spirits of those savages. And it was high time she should. For, through her faint proceedings against them, they had grown to that insolence, as to think of setting up for an independency on *England*. Nay, the presumption of that arch-rebel TYRONE, countenanced and abetted by *Spain*, seemed to threaten the queen with still further mischiefs. The extreme dishonour

honour and even peril of this situation roused her old age, at length, to the resolution of taking some effectual measures. The preparation was great, and suitable to the undertaking. It must, further, be owned, it succeeded; but so late, that she herself did not live to see the full effect of it. However, this success is reckoned among the glories of her reign. In the mean time, it is not considered that nothing but her ill policy, in suffering the disorders of that country to gather to a head, made way for this glory. I call it her *ill policy*, for unless it were rather owing to her excessive frugality [*b*] one can hardly help thinking

[*b*] Mr. CAMDEN owns that the *Irish* rebellion, which in the end became so dangerous, had been "encouraged by a slighting of it, and a gripple-handedness of *England*." [*Hist. of* ELIZ. B. iv.]— To the same purpose another eminent writer of that time—" Before the transmitting of the last great army, the forces sent over by Q. ELIZABETH were NOT of sufficient power to break and subdue all the *Irishry*." At last, however, " The extreme peril

ing she designed to perpetuate the *Irish* distractions. At least, it was agreeable to a favourite maxim of hers, to check, and not to suppress them. And I think it clear, from the manner of prosecuting the war, that, till this last alarm, she never was in earnest about putting an end to it.

SCOTLAND, indeed, demanded a more serious attention. Yet the weak distracted counsels of that court—a minor king—a captive queen—and the unsettled state of *France* itself, which defeated in a good degree the malice of the GUISES—were favourable circumstances.

peril of losing the kingdom; the dishonour and danger that might thereby grow to the crown of *England*; together with a just disdain conceived by that great-minded queen, that so wicked and ungrateful a rebel should prevail against her, who had ever been victorious against all her enemies, did move and almost ENFORCE her to send over that mighty army."
[Sir J. DAVIES, *Discovery of the State of Ireland*, p. 97. *Lond.* 1613.]

But to be fair with you (for I would appear in the light of a reasonable objector, not a captious wrangler); I allow her policy in this instance to have been considerable. She kept a watchful eye on the side of *Scotland*. And, though many circumstances concurred to favour her designs, it must be owned they were not carried without much care and some wisdom.

I UNDERSTAND the value of this concession, replied Dr. ARBUTHNOT. It must have been no common degree of both, that extorted it from you.

I DECLINE entering further, said Mr. ADDISON, into the public transactions of that reign; if it were only that, at this distance of time, it may be no easy matter to determine any thing of the policy, with which they were conducted. Only give me leave to add, as a FOURTH instance

ſtance of the favourable circumſtances of the time, "That the prerogative was then in its height, and that a patient people allowed the queen to uſe it on all occaſions." Hence the apparent vigour and firmneſs of her adminiſtration: and hence the opportunity (which is ſo rarely found in our country) of directing the whole ſtrength of the nation to any end of government, which the glory of the prince or the public intereſt required.

WHAT you impute to the high ſtrain of prerogative, returned Dr. ARBUTHNOT, might rather be accounted for from the ability of her government, and the wiſe means ſhe took to ſupport it. The principal of theſe was, by employing the GREATEST MEN in the ſeveral departments of her adminiſtration. Every kind of merit was encouraged by her ſmile [c],

or

[c] Sir ROBERT NAUNTON tells us, "The queen was never profuſe in delivering out of her treaſure; but paid her ſervants part in money, and the

or rewarded by her bounty. Virtue, she knew, would thrive best on its native stock, a generous emulation. This she promoted by all means; by her royal countenance, by a temperate and judicious praise, by the wisest distribution of her preferments. Hence would naturally arise that confidence in the queen's counsels and undertakings, which the servile awe of her prerogative could never have occasioned.

This is the true account of the loyalty, obedience, and fidelity, by which her servants were distinguished. And thus, in fact, it was that, throughout her kingdom, there was every where that reve-

the rest with GRACE; which, as the case stood, was then taken for good payment." [FRAGM. REG. p. 89.] And NAT. BACON to the same purpose, " A wise man, that was an eye-witness of HER actions, and those that succeeded to her, many times hath said, That a courtier might make a better meal of one good LOOK from her, than of a gift from some other." [DISC. P. ii. p. 266. *Lond.* 1651.]

rence

rence of authority [*d*], that sense of honour, that conscience of duty, in a word, that gracious simplicity of manners, which renders the age of ELIZABETH truly GOLDEN: as presenting the fairest picture of humanity, that is to be met with in the accounts of any people.

IT is true, as you say, interposed Mr. ADDISON, that this *picture is a fair one.* But of what is it a copy? Of the GENIUS of the time, or of the queen's virtues? You shall judge for yourself, after I

[*d*] This *reverence of authority,* one of the characteristics of that time, and which Mr. ADDISON presently accounts for, a great writer celebrates in these words—" It was an ingenuous uninquisitive time, when all the passions and affections of the people were lapped up in such an innocent and humble obedience, that there was never the least contestation nor capitulation with the queen, nor (though she very frequently consulted with her subjects) *any further reasons urged of her actions, than* HER OWN WILL." See a tract intitled THE DISPARITY, in Sir H. WOTTON's Remains, p. 46. supposed to have been written by the earl of CLARENDON.

have

have laid before you TWO remarkable events of that age, which could not but have the greatest effect on the public manners; I mean, THE REFORMATION OF RELIGION, and what was introductory of it, THE RESTORATION OF LETTERS. From these, as their proper sources, I would derive the ability and fidelity of ELIZABETH's good subjects.

THE passion for LETTERS was extreme. The novelty of these studies, the artifices that had been used to keep men from them, their apparent uses, and, perhaps, some confused notion of a certain diviner virtue than really belongs to them; these causes concurred to excite a curiosity in all, and determined those, who had leisure, as well as curiosity, to make themselves acquainted with the *Greek* and *Roman* learning. The ecclesiastics, who, for obvious reasons, would be the first and most earnest in their application to letters, were not the only

persons

persons transported with this zeal. The gentry and nobility themselves were seized with it. A competent knowledge of the old writers was looked upon as essential to a gentleman's education. So that *Greek* and *Latin* became as fashionable at court in those days, as *French* is in ours. ELIZABETH herself, which I wonder you did not put me in mind of, was well skilled in both [*e*]; they say, employed

[*e*] PAULUS HENTZNERUS, a learned *German*, who was in *England* in 1598, goes still further in his encomium on the queen's skill in languages. He tells us, that, " præterquam quód Græcè et Latinè eleganter est docta, tenet, ultra jam memorata idiomata, etiam Hispanicum, Scoticum, et Belgicum." See his ITINERARIUM.

But this was the general character of the great in that reign: at least, if we may credit Master WILLIAM HARRISON, who discourseth on the subject before us in the following manner: " This further is not to be omitted, to the singular commendation of both sorts and sexes of our courtiers here in *England*, that there are very few of them, which have not the use and skill of sundry speeches, beside an excellent vein of writing, before-time not regarded. Truly it is a rare thing with us now, to hear of a courtier which
hath

employed her leisure in making some fine translations out of either language. It is easy to see what effect this general attention to letters must have on the minds of the liberal and well-educated. And it was a happiness peculiar to that age, that learning, though cultivated with such zeal, had not as yet degenerated into pedantry: I mean, that, in those stirring and active times, it was cultivated, not so much for show, as use; and was not followed, as it soon came to be, to the exclusion of other generous and manly applications.

hath but his own language. And to say how many gentlewomen and ladies there are, that, beside sound knowledge of the *Greek* and *Latin* tongues, are thereto no less skilful in the *Spanish, Italian,* and *French,* or in some one of them, it resteth not in me: sith I am persuaded, that as the noblemen and gentlemen do surmount in this behalf, so these come very little or nothing behind them for their parts; which industry God continue, and accomplish that which otherwise is wanting." DE.CRIPT. of ENGLAND, p. 196.

CONSIDER,

CONSIDER, too, the effects, which the alterations in RELIGION had produced, As they had been lately made, as their importance was great, and as the benefits of the change had been earned at the expence of much blood and labour; all these confiderations begot a zeal for religion, which hardly ever appears under other circumftances. This zeal had an immediate and very fenfible effect on the morals of the Reformed. It improved them in every inftance;. especially as it produced a cheerful fubmiffion to the government, which had refcued them from their former flavery, and was ftill their only fupport againft the returning dangers of fuperftition. Thus religion, acting with all its power, and that, too, heightened by gratitude and even felf-intereft, bound obedience on the minds of men with the ftrongeft ties [*f*]. And luckily

[*f*] One of these *ties* was the *prejudice of education*; and fome uncommon methods were ufed to bind

luckily for the queen, this obedience was further secured to her by the high uncontroverted notions of royalty, which, at
bind it faſt on the minds of the people.—A book, called ΕΙΡΗΝΑΡΧΙΑ ſive ELIZABETH, was written in *Latin* verſe by one OCKLAND, containing the higheſt panegyrics on the queen's character and government, and ſetting forth the tranſcendent virtues of her miniſters. This book was enjoined by authority to be taught, as a claſſic author, in Grammar-ſchools, and was of courſe to be gotten by heart by the young ſcholars throughout the kingdom.

This was a matchleſs contrivance to imprint a ſenſe of loyalty on the minds of the people. And, though it flowed, as we are to ſuppoſe, from a tender regard, in the adviſers of it, for the intereſts of Proteſtantiſm in that reign; yet its uſes are ſo apparent in any reign, and under any adminiſtration, that nothing but the moderation of her ſucceſſors, and the reaſonable aſſurance of their miniſters that their own acknowledged virtues were a ſufficient ſupport to them, could have hindered the expedient from being followed.

But, though the ſtamp of public authority was wanting, private men have attempted, in ſeveral ways, to ſupply this defect. To inſtance only in one. The Proteſtant queen was to paſs for a mirror of *good government:* hence the Ειρηναρχια. Her ſucceſſor would needs be thought a mirror of *eloquence:* and hence the noble enterpriſe I am about to celebrate.

at that time, obtained amongst the people.

Lay all this together; and then tell me where is the wonder, that a people, now emerging out of ignorance; uncorrupted by wealth, and therefore undebauched by luxury; trained to obedience, and nurtured in simplicity; but, above all, caught with the love of learning and religion, while neither of them was worn for fashion-sake, or, what is worse, perverted to the ends of vanity or ambition;

brate. "Mr. GEORGE HERBERT (I give it in the grave historian's own words) being prælector in the rhetorique school in *Cambridge*, in 1618, passed by those fluent orators, that domineered in the pulpits of *Athens* and *Rome*, and insisted to read upon an oration of K. JAMES, which he analysed; shewed the concinnity of the parts; the propriety of the phrase; the height and power of it to move the affections; the style, UTTERLY UNKNOWN TO THE ANCIENTS; who could not conceive what kingly eloquence was, in respect of which those noted demagogi were but hirelings and triobolary rhetoricians." Bishop HACKET's Life of Archbishop WILLIAMS, p. 175.

where, I say, is the wonder that such a people should present so bright a picture of manners to their admiring panegyrist?

To be fair with you; it was one of those conjunctures, in which the active virtues are called forth, and rewarded. The dangers of the time had roused the spirit, and brought out all the force and genius, of the nation. A sort of enthusiasm had fired every man with the ambition of exerting the full strength of his faculties, which way soever they pointed, whether to the field, the closet, or the cabinet. Hence such a crop of soldiers, scholars, and statesmen had sprung up, as have rarely been seen to flourish together in any country. And as all owed their duty, it was the fashion of the times for all to bring their pretensions, to the court. So that, where the multitude of candidates was so great, it had been strange indeed, if an ordinary discretion had not furnished the queen with able

servants

servants of all sorts; and the rather, as her occasions loudly called upon her to employ the ablest.

I was waiting, said Dr. Arbuthnot, to see to what conclusion this career of your eloquence would at length drive you. And it hath happened in this case, as in most others where a favourite point is to be carried, that a zeal for it is indulged, though at the expence of some other of more importance. Rather than admit the personal virtues of the queen, you fill her court, nay, her kingdom, with heroes and sages: and so have paid a higher compliment to her reign, than I had intended.

To her *reign*, if you will, replied Mr. Addison, so far as regards the qualities and dispositions of her subjects: for I will not lessen the merit of this concession with you, by insisting, as I might, that their *manners*, respectable as they were,

were debased by the contrary, yet very consistent, vices of servility and insolence [g]; and their virtues of every kind deformed by barbarism. But, for the queen's own merit in the choice of her servants, I must take leave to declare my sentiments to you very plainly. It may be true, that she possessed a good degree of sagacity in discerning the natures and talents of men. It was the virtue by which, her admirers tell us, she

---

[g] A learned foreigner gives this character of the *English* at that time: "Angli, ut ADDICTE SERVIUNT, ità evecti ad dignitates priorem humilitatem INSOLENTIA rependunt." H. GROTII ANN. L. v. p. 95. *Amst.* 1657. Hence the propriety of those complaints, in our great poet, of,

"The whips and scorns of th' time,
Th' oppressor's wrong, the proud man's contumely,
THE INSOLENCE OF OFFICE."—

complaints so frequent, and so forcibly expressed by him, that we may believe he painted from his own observation, and perhaps experience, of this insolent misuse of authority. MEASURE FOR MEASURE, Act. II. Sc. vii.

was

was principally diftinguifhed. Yet, that the high fame of this virtue hath been owing to the felicity of the times, abounding in all forts of merit, rather than to her own judgment, I think clear from this circumftance, "That fome of the moft deferving of thofe days, in their feveral profeffions, had not the fortune to attract the queen's grace, in the proportion they might have expected." I fay nothing of poor SPENSER. Who has any concern for a poet [*b*]? But

[*b*] Yet it may feem probable, from this poet's conduct in *Ireland*, and his *View of the ftate of that country*, that his talents for *bufinefs* (fuch as CECIL himfelf muft have approved) were no lefs confiderable than for poetry. But he had ferved a difgraced man; and had drawn upon himfelf the admiration of the generous earl of *Effex*. So that, as the hiftorian expreffeth it, "by a fate which ftill follows poets, he always wreftled with poverty, though he had been fecretary to the lord GRAY, lord deputy of *Ireland*." All that remained for him was, "to be interred at *Weftminfter*, near to CHAUCER, at the charge of the earl of *Effex*; his hearfe being attended by poets, and mournful elegies and poems, with the pens that wrote them, thrown into his grave." CAMDEN, lib. iv.

if merit alone had determined her majesty's choice, it will hardly at this day admit a dispute, that the immortal Hooker and Bacon [*i*], at least, had ranked

[*i*] As to Sir Francis Bacon, the queen herself gave a very plausible reason, and doubtless much approved by the grave lawyers and other judicious persons of that time, for her neglect of this gentleman. "She did acknowledge (says the earl of *Essex* in a letter to Mr. Francis Bacon) you had a great wit, and an excellent gift of speech, and much other good learning. But in LAW, she rather thought you could make shew, to the utmost of your knowledge, than that you were deep." Mem. of Q. Elizabeth by Dr. Birch; to whom the public is exceedingly indebted for abundance of curious information concerning the history of those times.

If it be asked, how the queen came to form this conclusion, the answer is plain. It was from Mr. Bacon's having a GREAT WIT, an excellent GIFT OF SPEECH, and much other GOOD LEARNING.

It is true, Sir Francis Bacon himself gives another account of this matter. In a letter of advice to Sir George Villiers, he says, "In this dedication of yourself to the public, I recommend unto you principally that which I think was never done since I was born—that you countenance and encourage and advance ABLE MEN, in all kinds, degrees, and professions. For in the time of the Cecils, father ranked in another clafs than that, in which this great difcerner of fpirits thought fit to leave them.

And her character, continued he, in every other refpect is juft as equivocal. For having touched one part of it, I now turn from thefe general confiderations on the circumftances and genius of the time, to our more immediate fubject, the PERSONAL QUALITIES of ELIZABETH. Hitherto we have ftood aloof from the queen's perfon. But there is no proceeding a ftep further in this debate, unlefs you allow me a little more liberty. May I then be permitted to draw the veil of ELIZABETH'S court, and, by the lights which hiftory holds out to us, contemplate the myfteries, that were celebrated in that awful fanctuary?

ther and fon, ABLE MEN WERE BY DESIGN AND OF PURPOSE SUPPRESSED. CABALA, p. 57. ed. 1691.—But either way, indeed, the queen's character is equally faved.

AFTER so reverend a preface, replied Dr. ARBUTHNOT, I think you may be indulged in this liberty. And the rather, as I am not apprehensive that the honour of the illustrious queen is likely to suffer by it. The secrets of her cabinet-council, it may be, are not to be scanned by the profane. But it will be no presumption to step into the drawing-room.

YET I may be tempted, said Mr. ADDISON, to use a freedom in this survey of her majesty, that would not have been granted to her most favoured courtiers. As far as I can judge of her character, as displayed in that solemn scene of her court, she had some apparent VIRTUES, but more genuine VICES; which yet, in the public eye, had equally the fortune to reflect a lustre on her government.

Her gracious affability, her love of her people, her zeal for the national glory; were not these her more obvious and specious qualities? Yet I doubt they were not so much the proper effects of her nature, as her policy; a set of spurious virtues, begotten by the very necessity of her affairs.

For her AFFABILITY, she saw there was no way of being secure amidst the dangers of all sorts, with which she was surrounded, but by ingratiating herself with the body of the people. And, though in her nature she was as little inclined to this condescension as any of her successors, yet the expediency of this measure compelled her to save appearances. And it must be owned, she did it with grace, and even acted her part with spirit. Possibly, the consideration of her being a female actor, was no disadvantage to her.

But, when she had made this sacrifice to interest, her proper temper shewed itself clearly enough in the treatment of her nobles, and of all that came within the verge of the court. Her caprice, and jealousy, and haughtiness, appeared in a thousand instances. She took offence so easily, and forgave so difficultly, that even her principal ministers could hardly keep their ground, and were often obliged to redeem her favour by the lowest submissions. When nothing else would do, they sickened, and were even at death's door: from which peril, however, she would sometimes relieve them; but not till she had exacted from them, in the way of penance, a course of the most mortifying humiliations. Nay, the very ladies of her court had no way to maintain their credit with her, but by submitting patiently to the last indignities.

It is allowed, from the instances you have in view, returned Dr. ARBUTHNOT, that her nature was something high and imperious. But these sallies of passion might well enough consist with her general character of affability.

HARDLY, as I conceive, answered Mr. ADDISON, if you reflect that these sallies, or rather habits of passion, were the daily terror and vexation of all about her. Her very minions seemed raised for no other purpose, than the exercise of her ill-humour. They were encouraged, by her smile, to presume on the royal countenance, and then beaten down again in punishment of that presumption. But, to say the truth, the slavish temper of the time was favourable to such exertions of female caprice and tyranny. Her imperious father, all whose virtues she inherited, had taught her a sure way to quell the spirit of her nobles. They had

had been long used to stand in awe of the royal frown. And the people were pleased to find their betters ruled with so high a hand, at a time when they themselves were addressed with every expression of respect, and even flattery.

SHE even carried this mockery so far, that, as HARRINGTON observes well, "she converted her reign, through the perpetual love-tricks that passed between her and her people, into a kind of romance." And though that political projector, in prosecution of his favourite notion, supposes the queen to have been determined to these intrigues by observing, that the weight of property was fallen into the popular scale; yet we need look no further for an account of this proceeding, than the inherent haughtiness of her temper. She gratified the insolence of her nature, in neglecting, or rather beating down, her nobility, whose greatness might seem to

challenge

challenge refpect: while the court, fhe paid to the people, revolted her pride lefs, as paffing only upon herfelf, as well as others, for a voluntary act of affability. Juft as we every day fee very proud men carry it with much loftinefs towards their equals, or thofe who are raifed to fome nearnefs of degree to themfelves; at the fame time that they affect a fort of courtefy to fuch, as are confeffedly beneath them.

You fee, then, what her boafted affability comes to. She gave good words to her people, whom it concerned her to be well with, and whom her pride itfelf allowed her to *manage:* fhe infulted her nobles, whom fhe had in her power, and whofe abafement flattered the idea, fhe doted upon, of her own fuperiority and importance [k].

LET

[k] The lord MOUNTJOY [then Sir CHARLES BLOUNT], being of a military turn, had ftolen over into *France*, without the queen's knowledge, in order to

LET the queen's manner of treating her subjects be what it would, Dr. ARBUTHNOT said, it appears to have given no offence in those days, when the sincerity of her intentions was never questioned. Her whole life is a convincing argument, that she bore the most entire affection to her people.

HER LOVE OF HER PEOPLE, returned Mr. ADDISON hastily, is with me a very questionable virtue. For what account shall we give of the multitude of penal statutes, passed in her reign? Or, be-

---

to serve in *Bretagne*, under one of her generals. Upon his return, which was hastened too by her express command, "Serve me so again, said the queen, once more, and I will lay you fast enough for running. You will never leave, till you are knocked o'the head, as that inconsiderate fellow SIDNEY was. You shall go when I send you. In the mean time see that you lodge in the court, where you may FOLLOW YOUR BOOKS, READ, AND DISCOURSE OF THE WARS." Sir ROBERT NAUNTON'S FR. REG. in L. BERLEIGH.

cause

cause you will say, there was some colour for these; what excuse shall we make for her frequent grants of monopolies, so ruinous to the public wealth and happiness, and so perpetually complained of by her parliaments? You will say, she recalled them. She did so. But not till the general indignation had, in a manner, forced her to recall them. If by her *people*, be meant those of the poorer and baser sort only, it may be allowed, she seemed on all occasions willing to spare them. But for those of better rank and fortune, she had no such consideration. On the other hand, she contrived in many ways to pillage and distress them. It was the tameness of that time, to submit to every imposition of the sovereign. She had only to command her gentry on any service she thought fit, and they durst not decline it. How many of her wealthiest and best subjects did she impoverish by these means (though under colour, you may be sure, of her high favour);

vour); and sometimes by her very visits! I will not be certain, added he, that her visit to this pompous castle of her own LEICESTER, had any other intention.

But what, above all, are we to think of her vow of celibacy, and her obstinate refusal to settle the succession, though at the constant hazard of the public peace and safety?

You are hard put to it, I perceive, interrupted Dr. ARBUTHNOT, to impeach the character of the queen in this instance, when a few penal laws, necessary to the support of her crown in that time of danger; one wrong measure of her government, and that corrected; the ordinary use of her prerogative; and even her virginity, are made crimes of. But I am curious to hear what you have to object to her ZEAL FOR THE ENGLISH GLORY, carried so high in her reign; and the single point, as it seems to me, to which

which all her measures and all her counsels were directed.

The *English* glory, Mr. Addison said, may, perhaps, mean the state and independency of the crown. And then, indeed, I have little to object. But, in any other sense of the word, I have sometimes presumed to question with myself, if it had not been better consulted, by a more effectual assistance of the Reformed on the continent; by a more vigorous prosecution of the war against *Spain* [*l*];

[*l*] So good a judge of military matters, as Sir Walter Raleigh, was of this opinion with regard to the conduct of the *Spanish* war. "If the late queen would have believed her men of war, as she did her scribes, we had, in her time, beaten that great empire in pieces, and made their kings, kings of figs and oranges, as in old times. But *her majesty did all by halves*, and, by petty invasions, taught the *Spaniard* how to defend himself, and to see his own weakness; which, till our attempts taught him, was hardly known to himself." See his Works, vol. i. p. 273.—Raleigh, it may be said, was of the Cecil faction. But the men of war, of the Essex faction, talked exactly in the same strain; which shews that this might probably be the truth.

and,

and, as I hinted before, by a more complete reduction of *Ireland*. But say, we are no judges of those high matters. What glory accrued to the *English* name, by the insidious dealing with the queen of *Scots*; by the vindictive proceedings against the duke of *Norfolk*; by the merciless persecutions of the unhappy earl of *Essex*? The same spirit, you see, continued from the beginning of this reign to the end of it. And the observation is the better worth attending to, because some have excused the queen's treatment of Essex by saying, "That her nature, in that decline of life, was somewhat clouded by apprehensions; as the horizon, they observe, in the evening of the brightest day, is apt to be obscured by vapours [*m*]." As if this fanciful simile,

[*m*] See Sir HENRY WOTTON's *Parallel of the earl of Essex and duke of Buckingham*. The words are these: "He [the earl of *Essex*] was to wrestle with a queen's declining, or rather with her very setting age, as we may term it; which, besides other respects, is commonly even of itself the more umbratious

simile, which illustrates perhaps, could excuse, the perverseness of the queen's temper; or, as if that could deserve to pass for an incident of age, which operated through life, and so declares itself to have been the proper result of her nature.

You promised, interposed Dr. ARBUTHNOT, not to pry too closely into the secrets of the cabinet. And such I must needs esteem the points to be, which you have mentioned. But enough of these beaten topics. I would rather attend you in the survey you promised to take of her court, and of the princely qualities that adorned it. It is from what passes in the inside of his palace, rather than from some questionable public acts, that the real character of a prince is best determined. And there, me-

bratious and apprehensive; as for the most part all horizons are charged with certain vapours towards their evening." REMAINS, p. 11.

thinks,

thinks, you have a scene opened to you, that deserves your applause. Nothing appears but what is truly royal. Nobody knew better, than ELIZABETH, how to support the decorum of her rank. She presided in that high orb with the dignity of a great queen. In all emergencies of danger, she shewed a firmness, and on all occasions of ceremony, a magnificence, that commanded respect and admiration. Her very diversions were tempered with a severity becoming her sex and place, and which made her court, even in its lightest and gayest humours, a school of virtue.

THESE are the points, concluded he, I could wish you to speak to. The rest may be left to the judgment of the historian, or rather to the curiosity of the nice and critical politician.

You shall be obeyed, Mr. ADDISON said. I thought it not amiss to take off the

the glare of those applauded qualities, which have dazzled the public at a distance, by shewing that they were either feigned or over-rated. But I come now to unmask the real character of this renowned princess. I shall paint her freely indeed, but truly as she appears to me. And, to speak my mind at once, I think it is not so much to her virtues, which at best were equivocal, as to her very VICES, that we are to impute the popular admiration of her character and government.

I BEFORE took notice of the high, indecent PASSION, she discovered towards her courtiers. This fierceness of temper in the softer sex was taken for heroism; and, falling in with the slavish principles of the age, begot a degree of reverence in her subjects, which a more equal, that is, a more becoming, deportment would not have produced. Hence, she was better served than most of our princes,

princes, only because she was more feared; in other words, because she less deserved to be so. But high as she would often carry herself in this unprincely, I had almost said unwomanly, treatment of her servants; awing the men by her oaths, and her women by blows; it is still to be remembered, that she had a great deal of natural TIMIDITY in her constitution.

WHAT! interrupted Dr. ARBUTHNOT hastily, the magnanimous ELIZABETH a coward? I should as soon have expected that charge against CÆSAR himself, or your own MARLBOROUGH.

I DISTINGUISH, Mr. ADDISON said, betwixt a parade of courage, put on to serve a turn, and keep her people in spirits, and that true greatness of mind, which, in one word, we call *magnanimity*. For this last, I repeat it, she either had it not, or not in the degree in which it

has

has been ascribed to her. On the contrary, I see a littleness, a pusillanimity, in her conduct on a thousand occasions. Hence it was, that both to her people and such of the neighbouring states as she stood in awe of, she used an excessive hypocrisy, which, in the language of the court, you may be sure, was called policy. To the *Hollanders,* indeed, she could talk big; and it was not her humour to manage those, over whom she had gained an ascendant. This has procured her, with many, the commendation of a princely magnanimity. But, on the other hand, when discontents were apprehended from her subjects, or when *France* was to be diverted from any designs against her, no art was forgotten that might cajole their spirits with all the professions of cordiality and affection. Then she was *wedded,* that was the tender word, to her people: and then the interest of religion itself was sacrificed by this Proteſtant queen to her newly-perverted brother on the continent.

HER foible, in this reſpect, was no ſecret to her miniſters. But above all it was practiſed upon moſt ſucceſsfully by the Lord BURGHLEY; "for whom, as I have ſeen it obſerved, it was as neceſſary that there ſhould be treaſons, as for the ſtate that they ſhould be prevented [*n*]." Hence it was, that he was perpetually raiſing her fears, by the diſcovery of ſome plot, or, when that was wanting, by the propoſal of ſome law for her greater ſecurity. In ſhort, he was for ever finding, or making, or ſuggeſting, dangers. The queen, though ſhe would look big (for indeed ſhe was an excellent actreſs), ſtartled at the ſhadows of thoſe dangers, the ſlighteſt rumours. And to this convenient timidity of his miſtreſs, ſo conſtantly alarmed, and relieved in turn by this wily miniſter, was owing, in

[*n*] THE DISPARITY, p. 43.

a good

a good degree, that long and unrivalled intereſt, he held in her favour.

STILL, further, to this conſtitutional *fear* (which might be forgiven to her ſex, if it had not been ſo ſtrangely mixed with a more than maſculine ferocity in other inſtances) muſt be aſcribed thoſe favourite maxims of policy, which ran through her whole government. Never was prince more attached to the Machiavelian doctrine, DIVIDE ET IMPERA, than our ELIZABETH [*o*]. It made the ſoul of

[*o*] This account of her policy is confirmed by what we read in the DISPARITY, before cited. "That trick of countenancing and protecting factions (as that queen, almoſt her whole reign, did with ſingular and equal demonſtration of grace look upon ſeveral perſons of moſt diſtant wiſhes one towards another) was not the leaſt ground of much of her quiet and ſucceſs. And ſhe never doubted but that men, that were never ſo oppoſite in their good-will each to other, or never ſo diſhoneſt in their projectments for each other's confuſion, might yet be reconciled in their allegiance towards her. Inſomuch that, during her whole reign, ſhe never endeavoured to reconcile any perſonal differences in the

of her policies, domeſtic and foreign. She countenanced the two prevailing factions of the time. The Churchmen and Puritans divided her favour ſo equally, that her favourites were ſure to be the chiefs of the contending parties. Nay, her court was a conſtant ſcene of cabals and perſonal animoſities. She gave a ſecret, and ſometimes an open, countenance to theſe jealouſies. The ſame principle directed all her foreign [*p*] negociations.

the court, though the unlawful emulations of perſons of neareſt truſt about her, were ever like to overthrow ſome of her chiefeſt deſigns: *A policy, ſeldom entertained by princes, eſpecially if they have iſſues to ſurvive them.*" p. 46. Her own hiſtorian, it is true, ſeems a little ſhy of acknowledging this conduct of the queen, with regard to her nobility and miniſters. But he owns, " She now and then took a pleaſure (and not unprofitably) in the emulation and privy grudges of her women." CAMDEN's ELIZABETH, p. 79. fol. *Lond.* 1688.

[*p*] We find an intimation to this purpoſe, in a writer of credit, at leaſt with reſpect to the *Dutch* and *Ireland*—" Jam et *divulſam* Hiberniam, et in Batavis Angli militis *ſeditiones*, velut JUSSAS, erant qui exprobrarent." GROTII ANNAL. l. xii. p. 432.

AND

AND are you not aware, interrupted Dr. ARBUTHNOT, that this objected policy is the very topic that I, and every other admirer of the queen, would employ in commendation of her great ability in the art of government? It has been the fate of too many of our princes (and perhaps some late examples might be given) to be governed, and even insulted, by a prevailing party of their own subjects. ELIZABETH was superior to such attempts. She had no bye-ends to pursue. She frankly threw herself on her people. And, secure in their affection, could defeat at pleasure, or even divert herself with, the intrigues of this or that aspiring faction.

WE understand you, Mr. ADDISON replied; but when two parties are contending within a state, and one of them only in its true interest, the policy is a little extraordinary that should incline the sovereign to discourage *this*, from the poor ambition of controuling *that*, or, as you put it still worse, from the dangerous humour of playing with *both* parties. I say nothing of later times. I only ask, if it was indifferent, whether the counsels of the CECILS or of LEYCESTER were predominant in that reign? But I mentioned these things before, and I touch them again now, only to shew you, that this conduct, however it may be varnished over by the name of wisdom, had too much the air of fearful womanish intrigue, to consist with that heroical firmness and intrepidity, so commonly ascribed to queen ELIZABETH [*q*].

AND

[*q*] Something like this was observed of her disposition by Sir JAMES MELVIL. After having related to his mistress, the queen of *Scots*, the strong professions of friendship which the queen of *England* had made to him, " She [the queen of *Scots*] inquired, says he, whether I thought that queen meant truly towards her inwardly in her heart, as she appeared to do outwardly in her speech. I answered freely, that, in my judgment, there was neither plain
dealing,

AND what if, after all, I should admit, replied Dr. ARBUTHNOT, that, in the composition of a woman's courage, at least, there might be some scruples of discretion? Is there any advantage, worth contending for, you could draw from such a concession? Or, because you would be thought serious, I will put the matter more gravely. The arts of prudence, you arraign so severely, could not be taken for pusillanimity. They certainly were not, in her own time; for she was not the less esteemed or revered by all the nations of *Europe* on account of them. The most you can fairly conclude is, that she knew how to unite address with bravery, and that, on occasion, she could *dissemble* her high spirit. The difficulties

dealing, nor upright meaning; but great dissimulation, emulation, and FEAR, left her princely qualities should over-soon chace her from her kingdom," &c. MEMOIRS, p. 53.

of her situation obliged her to this management.

RATHER say at once, returned Mr, ADDISON, that the constant dissimulation, for which she was so famous, was assumed to supply the want of a better thing, which had rendered all those arts as unnecessary as they were ignoble.

BUT *haughtiness* and *timidity*, pursued he, were not the only vices that turned to good account in the queen's hands. She was frugal beyond all bounds of decorum in a prince, or rather AVARICIOUS beyond all reasonable excuse from the public wants and the state of her revenue. Nothing is more certain than this fact, from the allowance both of friends and enemies. It seems as if, in this respect, her father's example had not been sufficient; and that, to complete her character, she had incorporated

porated with many of his, the leading vice of her grandfather.

Here Dr. Arbuthnot could not contain himself; and the castle happening at that time, from the point where they stood, to present the most superb prospect, "Look there, said he, on the striking, though small, remnants of that grandeur you just now magnified so much; and tell me if, in your conscience, you can believe such grants are the signs, or were the effects, of avarice. For you are not to learn, that this palace before us is not the only one in the kingdom, which bears the memory of the queen's bounty to her servants.

Mr. Addison seemed a little struck with the earnestness of this address: "It is true, said he, the queen's fondness for one or two of her favourites made her sometimes lavish of her grants; especially of what cost her nothing, and did not, it seems,

seems, offend the delicacy of her scruples; I mean, of the *church-lands*. But at the same time her treasury was shut against her ambassadors and foreign ministers; who complain of nothing more frequently than the slenderness of their appointments, and the small and slow remittances that were made to them. This frugality (for I must not call it by a worse name) distressed the public service on many occasions [r]; and would have done it on more, if the zeal of her trusty

[r] Secretary WALSINGHAM, in a letter to the queen, *Sept.* 2, 1581, amongst other things to the same purpose, has the following words—" Remember, I humbly beseech your majesty, *the respect of charges hath lost Scotland:* and I would to God I had no cause to think, that *it might put your highness in peril of the loss of England*."—" And even the Lord Treasurer himself (we are told) in a letter still extant in the paper-office, written in the critical year 1588, while the *Spanish* armada was expected against *England*, excuses himself to Sir EDWARD STAFFORD, then embassador in *France*, for not writing to him oftener, *on account of her majesty's unwillingness to be at the expence of messengers*." Sir T. EDMONDE's State-papers, by Dr. BIRCH, p. 21.

servants

servants had not been content to carry it on at the expence of their own fortunes. How many instances might be given of this, if ONE were not more than sufficient, and which all posterity will remember with indignation!

You speak of WALSINGHAM, interposed Dr. ARBUTHNOT. But were it not more candid to impute the poverty of that minister to his own generous contempt of riches, which he had doubtless many fair occasions of procuring to himself, than to any designed neglect of him by his mistress?

THE candour, returned Mr. ADDISON, must be very extraordinary, that can find an excuse for the queen in a circumstance that doubles her disgrace. But be it as you pretend. The uncommon moderation of the man shall be a cover to the queen's parsimony. It was not, we will say, for this wise princess to provoke

voke an appetite for wealth in her servants: it was enough that she gratified it, on proper occasions, where she found it already raised. And in this proceeding, no doubt, she was governed by a tender regard for their honour, as well as her own interest. For how is her great secretary ennobled, by filling a place in the short list of those worthies, who, having lived and died in the service of their countries, have left not so much as a pittance behind them, to carry them to their graves! All this is very well. But when she had indulged this humour in one or two of her favourites, and suffered them, for example's sake, to ascend to these heights of honour, it was going, methinks, a little too far, to expect the same delicacy of virtue in all her courtiers. Yet it was not her fault, if most of them did not reap this fame of illustrious poverty, as well as WALSINGHAM. She dealt by them, indeed, as if
she

she had ranked poverty, as well as celibacy, among the cardinal virtues.

In the mean time, I would not deny that she had a princely fondness for shew and appearance. She took a pride in the brilliancy of her court. She delighted in the large trains of her nobility. She required to be royally entertained by them. And she thought her honour concerned in the figure they made in foreign courts, and in the wars. But, if she loved this pomp, she little cared to furnish the expence of it. She considered in good earnest (as some have observed, who would have the observation pass for a compliment [*s*]) *the purses of her*

[*s*] One of these complaisant observers was the writer of *the Description of England*, who, speaking of the variety of the queen's houses, checks himself with saying, " But what shall I need to take upon me to repeat all, and tell what houses the queen's majesty hath? Sith ALL IS HIRS; and when it pleaseth hir in the summer season to recreate hirself abroad, and view the state of the countrie, and hear

her subjects as her own; and seemed to reckon on their being always open to her on any occasion of service, or even ceremony. She carried this matter so far, that the very expences of her wars were rather defrayed out of the private purses of her nobility, than the public treasury. As if she had taken it for a part of her *prerogative* to impoverish her nobles at pleasure; or rather, as if she had a mind to have it thought that one of their *privileges* was, to be allowed to ruin themselves from a zeal to her service.

But the queen's avarice, proceeded he, did not only appear from her excessive parsimony in the management of the public treasure, but from her rapa-

the complaints of hir unjust officers or substitutes, *every nobleman's house is hir palace,* where she continueth during pleasure, and till she returne againe to some of hir owne; in which she remaineth as long as pleaseth hir." p. 196.

city

city in getting what she could from particulars into her privy purse. Hence it was that all offices, and even personal favours, were in a manner set to sale. For it was a rule with her majesty, to grant no suit but for a reasonable consideration. So that whoever pretended to any place of profit or honour, was sure to send a jewel, or other rich present beforehand, to prepare her mind for the entertainment of his petition. And to what other purpose was it that she kept her offices so long vacant, but to give more persons an opportunity of winning a preference in her favour; which for the most part inclined to those who had appeared, in this interval, to deserve it best? Nay, the slightest disgust, which she frequently took on very frivolous occasions, could not be got over but by the reconciling means of some valuable or well-fancied present. And, what was most grievous, she sometimes accepted the present, without remitting the offence.

I REMEMBER a ridiculous instance of this sort. When the Lady LEICESTER wanted to obtain the pardon of her unfortunate son, the Lord ESSEX, she presented the queen with an exceeding rich gown, to the value of above an hundred pounds. She was well pleased with the gift, but thought no more of the pardon. We need not, after this, wonder at what is said of her majesty's leaving a prodigious quantity of jewels and plate behind her, and even a *crowded wardrobe*. For so prevalent was this thrifty humour in the queen's highness, that she could not persuade herself to part with so much as a cast-gown to any of her servants [t].

---

[t] Perhaps they had no need of such favours. It seems as if they had provided for themselves another way. One of her ladies, the Lady EDMONDES, had been applied to for her interest with the queen in

You allow yourself to be very gay, replied Dr. ARBUTHNOT, on this foible of the great queen. But one thing you forget,

in a certain affair of no great moment, then depending in the Court of Chancery. The person, commissioned to transact this matter with her ladyship, had offered her 100*l.* which she treated *as too small a sum.* The relater of this fact adds—" This ruffianry of causes I am daily more and more acquainted with, and see the manner of dealing, which cometh of the queen's *straitness* to give these women, whereby they presume thus to grange and truck causes." See a letter in MEM. of Q. ELIZABETH, by Dr. BIRCH, vol. i. p. 354. But this 100*l.* as the virtuous Lady EDMONDEs says, was *a small sum.* It appears, that bishop FLETCHER, on his translation to *London,* " bestowed in allowances and gratifications to divers attendants [indeed we are not expressly told, they were *female*] about her majesty, the sum of 3100*l.* which money was given by him, for the most part of it, *by her majesty's direction and special appointment.*" Mem. vol. ii. p. 113. And the curiosity is, to find this minute of episcopal *gratifications* in a petition presented to the queen herself, " To move her majesty in commiseration towards the orphans of this bishop."—However, to do the ladies justice, the contagion of bribery was so general in that reign, that the greatest men in the court were infected by it. The lord-keeper PUCKERING, forget, that it never biassed her judgment so far as to prevent a fit choice of her servants on all occasions [*u*]. And, as to her wary management of the public revenue, which you take a pleasure to exaggerate, this, methinks, is a venial fault in a prince, who could not, in her circumstances, have provided for the expences of government, but by the nicest and most attentive œconomy.

PUCKERING, it seems, had a finger in the affair of the 100*l.*; nay, himself speaks to the lady to get him commanded by the queen to favour the suit. And we are told, that Sir W. RALEIGH had no less than 10,000*l.* for his interest with the queen on a certain occasion, after having been invited to this service by the finest letter that ever was written.— Indeed it is not said how much of this secret service money went *in allowances and gratifications to the attendants about the queen's majesty*, vol. ii. p. 497.

[*u*] Lord BACON made the same excuse for *his* bribery; as he had learnt, perhaps, the trade itself from his royal mistress. It was a rule with this great chancellor, "Not to sell injustice, but never to let justice go scot-free."

I UNDERSTAND, said Mr. ADDISON, the full force of that confideration; and believe it was that *attention* principally, which occafioned the popularity of her reign, and the high efteem, in which the wifdom of her government is held to this day. The bulk of her fubjects were, no doubt, highly pleafed to find themfelves fpared on all occafions of expence. And it ferved, at the fame time, to gratify their natural envy of the great, to find that *their* fortunes were firft and principally facrificed to the public fervice. Nay, I am not fure that the very rapacity of her nature, in the fale of her offices, was any objection with the people at large, or even the lower gentry of the kingdom. For thefe, having no pretenfions themfelves to thofe offices, would be well enough pleafed to fee them, not *beftowed* on their betters, but dearly purchafed by them. And then this traffic at court furnifhed the inferior gentry with a pretence for making the most of their magistracies. This practice at least must have been very notorious amongst them, when a facetious member of the lower house could define a justice of peace to be, " A living creature, that for half a dozen of chickens, will dispense with a whole dozen of penal statutes [*w*]." But, however this be, the queen's ends, in every view, were abundantly answered. She enriched herself: she gained the affections of the people, and depressed and weakened the nobility, And by all these ways she effectually provided for, what she had ever most at heart, her own supreme and uncontrolled authority.

[*w*] See *Hist. Collections*, by H. TOWNSHEND, Esq; p. 268. *Lond.* 1680.—The lord-keeper too, in a speech in the star-chamber, confirms this charge on the country justices. "The thirst, says he, after this authority, proceedeth from nothing but an ambitious humour of gaining of reputation amongst their neighbours; that still, when they come home, *they may be presented with presents."* Ibid. p. 355.

AND is that to be wondered at in a great prince? returned Dr. ARBUTHNOT. Or, to take the matter in the light you place it, what if the queen had so much of her sex [*] and family in her disposition, as to like well enough to have her own way, is this such a crime as you would make of it? If she loved power, it was not to make a wanton or oppressive use of it. And if all princes knew as well to bound their own wills, as she did, we should not much complain of their

[*] When the queen declared to Sir JAMES MELVIL her resolution of virginity, "I know the truth of that, madam; (said he) you need not tell it me. Your majesty thinks, if you were married, you would be but queen of *England*; and now you are both king and queen. *I know your spirit cannot endure a commander.*" MEM. p. 49. This was frank. But Sir JAMES MELVIL was too well seen in courts to have used this language, if he had not understood it would be welcome. Accordingly, the queen's highness did not seem displeased with the imputation.

impatience to be under the control of their subjects.

I AM sorry, said Mr. ADDISON, that the acts of her reign will not allow me to come into this opinion of her moderation. On the other hand, her government appears to me, in many instances, OPPRESSIVE, and highly prejudicial to the antient rights and privileges of her people. For what other construction can we make of her frequent interposition to restrain the counsels of their representatives in parliament: threatening some, imprisoning others, and silencing all with the thunder of her prerogative? Or, when she had suffered their counsels to ripen into bills, what shall we say of her high and mighty rejection of them, and that not in single and extraordinary cases, but in matters of ordinary course, and by dozens? I pass by other instances. But was her *moderation* seen in dilapidating the revenues of the church; of that church,

church, which she took under the wing of her supremacy, and would be thought to have sheltered from all its enemies [*y*]? The honest archbishop PARKER, I have

[*y*] This was a common topic of complaint against the queen, or at least her ministers, and gave occasion to that reproof of the poet SPENCER, which the persons concerned could hardly look upon as very decent,

" Scarce can a bishoprick forepass them bye
But that it must be gelt in privity."
Mother HUBBARD's *Tale*.

But a bishop of that time carries the charge still further. In one of his sermons at court before the queen, " Parsonages and vicarages, says he, seldom pass now-a-days from the patron, but either for the lease, or the present money. Such merchants are broken into the church of God, a great deal more intolerable than were they, whom CHRIST whipped out of the temple."—This language is very harsh, and surely not deserved by the Protestant patrons of those days, who were only, as we may suppose, for reducing the church of CHRIST to its pure and primitive state of indigence and suffering. How edifying is it to hear St. PAUL speak of his being—*In hunger and thirst, in fastings often, in cold and nakedness!* And how perfectly reformed would our church be, if its ministers were but once more in this blessed apostolical condition!

heard,

heard, ventured to remonstrate against this abuse, the cognizance of which came so directly within his province. But to what effect, may be gathered, not only from the continuance of these depredations, but her severe reprehension of another of her bishops, whom she threatened with an oath to UNFROCK—that was her majesty's own word—if he did not immediately give way to her princely extortions.

IT may be hardly worth while to take notice of smaller matters. But who does not resent her capricious tyranny, in disgracing such of her servants as presumed to deviate, on any pretence, from her good pleasure; nay, such as gave an implicit obedience to her will, if it stood with her interest to disgrace them? Something, I know, may be said to excuse the proceedings against the queen of *Scots*. But the fate of DAVISON will
reflect

reflect eternal dishonour on the policy, with which that measure was conducted.

I RUN over these things hastily, continued Mr. ADDISON, and in no great order: but you will see what to conclude from these hints; which taken together, I believe, may furnish a proper answer to the most considerable parts of your apology.

To sum it up in few words. Those two great events of her time, THE ESTABLISHMENT OF THE REFORMATION, and THE TRIUMPH OVER THE POWER OF SPAIN, cast an uncommon lustre on the reign of ELIZABETH. Posterity, dazzled with these obvious successes, went into an excessive admiration of her personal virtues. And what has served to brighten them the more, is the place in which we chance to find her, between the bigot queen on the one hand, and the pedant king on the other.

No wonder then that, on the first glance, her government should appear able, and even glorious. Yet, in looking into particulars, we find that much is to be attributed to fortune, as well as skill; and that her glory is even lessened by considerations, which, on a careless view, may seem to augment it. The difficulties, she had to encounter, were great. Yet these very difficulties, of themselves, created the proper means to surmount them. They sharpened the wits, inflamed the spirits, and united the affections, of a whole people. The name of her great enemy on the continent, at that time, carried terror with it. Yet his power was, in reality, much less than it appeared. The *Spanish* empire was corrupt and weak, and tottered under its own weight. But this was a secret even to the *Spaniard* himself. In the mean time, the confidence, which the opinion of great strength inspires, was a favourable circumstance. It occasioned a remiss-
nefs

ness and neglect of counsel on one side, in proportion as it raised the utmost vigilance and circumspection on the other. But this was not all. The religious feuds in the Low Countries—the civil wars in *France*—the distractions of *Scotland*—all concurred to advance the fortunes of ELIZABETH. Yet all had, perhaps, been too little in that grand crisis of her fate, and, as it fell out, of her glory, if the conspiring elements themselves had not fought for her.

SUCH is the natural account of her foreign triumphs. Her domestic successes admit as easy a solution. Those external dangers themselves, the genius of the time, the state of religious parties, nay, the very factions of her court, all of them directly, or by the slightest application of her policy, administered to her greatness. Such was the condition of the times, that it forced her to assume the resemblance, at least, of some popular

lar *virtues*: and so singular her fortune, that her very *vices* became as respectable, perhaps more useful to her reputation, than her virtues. She was vigilant in her counsels; careful in the choice of her servants; courteous and condescending to her subjects. She appeared to have an extreme tenderness for the interests, and an extreme zeal for the honour, of the nation. This was the bright side of her character; and it shone the brighter from the constant and imminent dangers, to which she was exposed. On the other hand, she was choleric, and imperious; jealous, timid, and avaricious: oppressive, as far as she durst; in many cases capricious, in some tyrannical. Yet these vices, some of them sharpened and refined her policy, and the rest, operating chiefly towards her courtiers and dependents, strengthened her authority, and rooted her more firmly in the hearts of the people. The mingled splendour of these
qualities,

qualities, good and bad (for even her worst had the luck, when seen but on one side, or in well-disposed lights, to look like good ones) so far dazzled the eyes of all, that they did not, or would not, see many outrageous acts of tyranny and oppression.

AND thus it hath come to pass that, with some ability, more cunning, and little real virtue, the name of ELIZABETH is, by the concurrence of many accidental causes, become the most revered of any in the long roll of our princes. How little she merited this honour, may appear from this slight sketch of her character and government. Yet, when all proper abatement is made in both, I will not deny her to have been a great, that is, a *fortunate*, queen; in this, perhaps, the most fortunate, that she has attained to so unrivalled a glory with so few pretensions to deserve it.

AND

AND so, replied Dr. ARBUTHNOT, you have concluded your invective in full form, and rounded it, as the antient orators used to do, with all the advantage of a peroration. But, setting aside this trick of eloquence, which is apt indeed to confound a plain man, unused to such artifices, I see not but you have left the argument much as you took it up; and that I may still have leave to retain my former reverence for the good old times of queen ELIZABETH. It is true, she had some foibles. You have spared, I believe, none of them. But, to make amends for these defects, let but the history of her reign speak for her, I mean in its own artless language, neither corrupted by flattery, nor tortured by invidious glosses; and we must ever conceive of her, I will not say as the most faultless, perhaps not the most virtuous, but surely the most able, and, from the

splendor

splendor of some leading qualities, the most glorious of our *English* monarchs.

To give you my notion of her in few words.—For the dispute, I find, must end, as most others usually do, in the simple representation of our own notions.—She was discreet, frugal, provident, and sagacious: intent on the pursuit of her great ends, *the establishment of religion*, and *the security and honour of her people*: prudent in the choice of the best *means* to effect them, the employment of able servants, and the management of the public revenue: dexterous at improving all advantages which her own wisdom or the circumstances of the times gave her: fearless and intrepid in the execution of great designs, yet careful to unite the deepest foresight with her magnanimity. If she seemed AVARICIOUS, let it be considered that the nicest frugality was but necessary in her situation: if IMPERIOUS, that a female government

vernment needed to be made respectable by a shew of authority: and if at any time OPPRESSIVE, that the *English* constitution, as it then stood, as well as her own nature, had a good deal of that bias.

IN a word, let it be remembered, that she had the honour of ruling [z], perhaps of forming, the wisest, the bravest, the most virtuous people, that have adorned any age or country; and that she advanced the glory of the *English* name and that of her own dignity to a height, which has no parallel in the annals of our nation.

[z] It was this circumstance that seemed to weigh most with the Lord Chancellor BACON; who, in his short tract, *In felicem memoriam* ELIZABETHÆ, saith, " Illud cogitandum censeo, in quali populo imperium tenuerit: si enim in Palmyrenis, aut Asiâ imbelli et molli regnum sortita esset, minùs mirandum fuisset—verùm in ANGLIA, *natione ferocissimâ et bellicosissimâ* omnia ex nutu fœminæ moveri et cohiberi potuisse, SUMMAM MERITO ADMIRATIONEM HABET."

Mr. Digby, who had been very attentive to the courſe of this debate, was a little diſappointed with the concluſion of it. He thought to have ſettled his judgment of this reign by the information, his two friends ſhould afford him. But he found himſelf rather perplexed by their altercations, than convinced by them. He owned, however, the pleaſure they had given him; and ſaid, he had profited ſo much at leaſt by the occaſion, that, for the future, he ſhould conceive with ſomething leſs reverence of the great queen, and ſhould proceed with leſs prejudice to form his opinion of her character and adminiſtration.

Mr. Addison did not appear quite ſatisfied with this ſceptical concluſion; and was going to enforce ſome things, which he thought had been touched too ſlightly, when Dr. Arbuthnot took notice

notice that their walk was now at an end; the path, they had taken, having by this time brought them round again to the walls of the caftle. Befides, he faid, he found himfelf much wearied with this exercife; though the warmth of debate, and the opportunities he took of refting himfelf at times, had kept him from complaining of it. He propofed, therefore, getting into the coach as foon as poffible; where, though the converfation was in fome fort refumed, there was nothing material enough advanced on either fide to make it neceffary for me to continue this recital any further.

DIALOGUE V.

On the CONSTITUTION of the ENGLISH Government.

SIR JOHN MAYNARD, MR. SOMERS, BISHOP BURNET [a].

TO DR. TILLOTSON.

THOUGH the principles of nature and common sense do fully authorise resistance to the civil magistrate in extreme cases, and of course justify the

[a] The subject of these Dialogues, on *the English Constitution*, is the most important in *English* politics. —To cite all the passages from our best antiquaries and historians, out of which this work was formed, and which lay before the writer in composing it, would swell this volume to an immoderate size. It is enough to say, that nothing *material* is advanced in the course of the argument, but on the best authority.

late Revolution to every candid and difpaſſionate man; yet I am ſenſible, my excellent friend, there are many prejudices which hinder the glorious proceedings in that affair from being ſeen in their true light. The principal of them, indeed, are founded on falſe ſyſtems of policy, and thoſe tied down on the conſciences of men by wrong notions of religion. And ſuch as theſe, no doubt, through the experience of a better government, and a juſter turn of thinking, which may be expected to prevail in our times, will gradually fall away of themſelves.

But there is another ſet of notions on this ſubject, not ſo eaſy to be diſcredited, and which are likely to keep their hold on the minds even of the more ſober and conſiderate ſort of men. For whatever advantage the cauſe of liberty may receive from general reaſonings on the origin and nature of civil government, the

the greater part of our countrymen will confider, and perhaps rightly, the inquiry into the conftitution of *their* own government, as a queftion of FACT; that muft be tried by authorities and precedents only; and decided at laft by the evidence of hiftorical teftimony, not by the concluſions of philofophy or political fpeculation.

Now, though we are agreed that this way of managing the controverfy muft, when fully and fairly purfued, be much in favour of the new fettlement, yet neither, I think, is it for every man's handling, nor is the evidence refulting from it of a nature to compel our affent. The argument is formed on a vaft variety of particulars, to be collected only from a large and intimate acquaintance with the antiquities, laws, and ufages of the kingdom. Our printed hiftories are not only very fhort and imperfect; but the original records, which the curious have in their poffeffion, are either fo obfcure or fo fcanty, that a willing adverfary hath always in readinefs fome objection, or fome cavil at leaft, to oppofe to the evidence that may be drawn from them. Befides, appearances, even in the plaineft and moft unqueftioned parts of our hiftory, are fometimes fo contradictory; arifing either from the tyranny of the prince, the neglect of the people, or fome other circumftance of the times; and, to crown all, the queftion itfelf hath been fo involved by the difputations of prejudiced and defigning men; that the more intelligent inquirer is almoft at a lofs to determine for himfelf, on which fide the force of evidence lies.

On this account I have frequently thought with myfelf, that a right good CONSTITUTIONAL HISTORY of *England* would be the nobleft fervice that any man, duly qualified for the execution of fuch a work, could render to his country. For

For though, as I said, the subject be obscure in itself, and perplexed by the subtilties which contending parties have invented for the support of their several schemes; yet, from all I have been able to observe in the course of my own reading, or conversation, there is little doubt but that the form of the *English* government hath, at all times, been FREE. So that, if such a history were drawn up with sufficient care out of our authentic papers and public monuments, it would not only be matter of entertainment to the curious, but the greatest security to every *Englishman* of his religious and civil rights. For what can be conceived more likely to preserve and perpetuate these rights, than the standing evidence which such a work would afford, of the genuine spirit and temper of the constitution? Of the principles of freedom [*b*],

on

[*b*] That is, of the *feudal law:* which was one of the subjects explained by the bishop to his royal pupil the duke of *Gloucester*. " I acquainted him,
says

on which it was formed, and on which it hath been continually and uniformly conducted? Our youth, who at present amuse themselves with little more than the military part of our annals, would then have an easy opportunity of seeing to the bottom of all our civil and domestic broils. They would know on what pretences the PREROGATIVE of our kings hath sometimes aspired to exalt itself above control; and would learn to revere the magnanimity of their forefathers, who as constantly succeeded in their endeavours to reduce it within the ancient limits and boundaries of the LAW. In a word, they would no longer rest on the surface and outside, as it were, of the *English* affairs, but would penetrate the interior parts of our constitution; and

says he, with all the great revolutions that had been in the world, and gave him a copious account of the *Greek* and *Roman* histories, and of PLUTARCH's lives: the last thing I explained to him was the Gothic constitution, and the BENEFICIARY AND FEUDAL LAWS." [HIST. *of his own Times*, vol. iv. p. 357. *Edinb.* 1753.]

furnish

furnish themselves with a competent degree of civil and political wisdom; the most solid fruit that can be gathered from the knowledge and experience of past times.

AND I am ready to think that such a provision as this, for the instruction of the *English* youth, may be the more requisite, on account of that limited indeed, yet awful form of government, under which we live. For, besides the name, and other ensigns of majesty, in common with those who wear the most despotic crown, the whole execution of our laws, and the active part of government, is in the hands of the prince. And this preeminence gives him so respectable a figure in the eyes of his subjects, and presents him so constantly, and with such lustre of authority, to their minds, that it is no wonder they are sometimes disposed to advance him from the rank of first magistrate giftrate of a free people, into that of supreme and fole arbiter of the laws.

So that, unlefs thefe prejudices are corrected by the knowledge of our conftitutional hiftory, there is conftant reafon to apprehend, not only that the royal authority may ftretch itfelf beyond due bounds; but may grow, at length, into that enormous tyranny, from which this nation hath been at other times fo happily, and now of late fo wonderfully, redeemed.

But I fuffer myfelf to be carried by thefe reflexions much further than I defigned. I would only fay to you, that, having fometimes reflected very ferioufly on this fubject, it was with the higheft pleafure I heard it difcourfed of the other day by two of the moft accomplifhed lawyers of our age: the venerable Sir John Maynard, who, for a long courfe of years, hath maintained the

full

full credit and dignity of his profession; and Mr. SOMERS, who, though a young man, is rising apace, and with proportionable merits, into all the honours of it.

I WAS very attentive, as you may suppose, to the progress of this remarkable conversation; and, as I had the honour to bear a full share in it myself, I may the rather undertake to give you a particular account of it. I know the pleasure it will give you to see a subject, you have much at heart, and which we have frequently talked over in the late times, thoroughly canvassed, and cleared up, as I think it must be, to your entire satisfaction.

It was within a day or two after that great event, so pleasing to all true *Englishmen*, THE CORONATION OF THEIR MAJESTIES [c], that Mr. SOMERS and I went, as we sometimes used, to pass an

[c] On *April* 11, 1689.

evening with our excellent friend, my Lord Commiffioner [*d*]. I fhall not need to attempt his character to you, who know him fo well. It is enough to fay, that his faculties and fpirits are, even in this maturity of age, in great vigour. And it feems as if this joyful Revolution, fo agreeable to his hopes and principles, had given a frefh fpring and elafticity to both.

THE converfation of courfe turned on the late auguft ceremony; the mention of which awakened a fort of rapture in the good old man, which made him overflow in his meditations upon it. Seeing us in admiration of the zeal, which tranfported him, " Bear with me, faid he, my young friends. Age, you know, hath its privilege. And it may be, I ufe it fomewhat unreafonably. But I, who have feen the prize of liberty contend-

[*d*] Of the great feal—The other lawyers in commiffion were KECK and RAWLINSON.

ing

ing for through half a century, to find it obtained at laſt by a method ſo ſure, and yet ſo unexpected, do you think it poſſible that I ſhould contain myſelf on ſuch an occaſion? Oh, if he had lived with me in thoſe days when ſuch mighty ſtruggles were made for public freedom, when ſo many wiſe counſels miſcarried, and ſo many generous enterpriſes concluded but in the confirmation of lawleſs tyranny; if, I ſay, ye had lived in thoſe days, and now at length were able to contraſt with me, to the tragedies that were then acted, this ſafe, this bloodleſs, this complete deliverance: I am miſtaken, if the youngeſt of you could reprove me for this joy, which makes me think I can never ſay enough on ſo delightful a ſubject.

BP. BURNET.

REPROVE you, my lord? Alas! we are neither of us ſo unexperienced in what hath paſſed of late in theſe kingdoms, as not to rejoice with you to the utmoſt

utmost for this astonishing deliverance. You know, I might boast of being among the first that wished for, I will not say projected, the measures by which it hath been accomplished. And for Mr. SOMERS, the church of *England* will tell.——

MR. SOMERS.

I CONFESS, my warmest wishes have ever gone along with those who conducted this noble enterprise. And I pretend to as sincere a pleasure as any man, in the completion of it. Yet, if it were not unreasonable at such a time, I might be tempted to mention one circumstance, which, I know not how, a little abates the joy of these triumphant gratulations.

SIR J. MAYNARD.

Is not the settlement then to your mind? Or hath any precaution been neglected, which you think necessary for the more effectual security of our liberties?

MR.

MR. SOMERS.

NOT that. I think the provision for the people's right as ample as needs be desired. Or, if any further restrictions on the crown be thought proper, it will now be easy for the people, in a regular parliamentary way, to effect it. What I mean is a consideration of much more importance.

BP. BURNET.

THE pretended prince of WALES, you think, will be raising some disturbance, or alarm at least, to the new government. I believe, I may take upon me to give you perfect satisfaction upon that subject [e].

MR. SOMERS.

STILL your conjectures fall short or wide of my meaning. Our new MAGNA

---

[e] This was a favourite subject with our good bishop; and how qualified he was to discuss it, even in its minutest particularities, may be learnt from his history at large.

CHARTA, as I love to call the *Declaration of rights*, seems a sufficient barrier against any future encroachments of the CROWN. And I think, the pretended prince of WALES, whatever be determined of his birth, a mere phantom, that may amuse, and perhaps disquiet, the weaker sort for a while; but, if left to itself [*f*], will soon vanish out of the minds of the PEOPLE. Not but I allow that even so thin a pretence as this may, some time or other, be conjured up to disturb the government. But it must be, when a certain set of principles are called in aid to support it. And, to save you the further trouble of guessing, I shall freely tell you, what those *principles* are.—You will see, in them, the ground of my present fears and apprehensions.

[*f*] It was not thus *left to itself*, but was nursed and fostered with great care by the preachers of *divine indefeasible hereditary right*, in this and the following reign.

IT

It might be imagined that so necessary a Revolution, as that which hath taken place, would sufficiently approve itself to all reasonable men. And it appears, in fact, to have done so, now that the public injuries are fresh, and the general resentment of them strong and lively. But it too often happens, that when the evil is once removed, it is presently forgotten: and in matters of government especially, where the people rarely think till they are made to feel, when the grievance is taken away, the false system easily returns, and sometimes with redoubled force, which had given birth to it.

BP. BURNET.

One can readily admit the principles. But the conclusion, you propose to draw from them—

MR. SOMERS.

This very important one, "That, if the late change of government was brought

brought about, and can be defended only, on the principles of liberty; the settlement, introduced by it, can be thought secure no longer than while those principles are rightly understood, and generally admitted."

BP. BURNET.

But what reason is there to apprehend that these principles, so commonly professed and publickly avowed, will not continue to be kept up in full vigour?

MR. SOMERS.

Because, I doubt, they are so commonly and publickly avowed, only to serve a present turn; and not because they come from the heart, or are entertained on any just ground of conviction.

BP. BURNET.

Very likely: and considering the pains that have been taken to possess the minds of men with other notions of government,

vernment, the wonder, is, how they came to be entertained at all. Yet surely the experience of better times may be expected to do much. Men will of course think more juftly on thefe fubjects in proportion as they find themfelves more happy. And thus the principles, which, as you fay, were firft pretended to out of neceffity, will be followed out of choice, and bound upon them by the conclufions of their own reafon.

MR. SOMERS.

I wish your lordfhip be not too fanguine in thefe expectations. It is not to be conceived how infenfible the people are to the bleffings they enjoy, and how eafily they forget their paft miferies. So that, if their principles have not taken deep root, I would not anfwer for their continuing much longer than it ferved their purpofe to make a fhew of them.

SIR J. MAYNARD.

I MUST confess, that all my experience of mankind inclines me to this opinion. I could relate to you some strange instances of the sort, Mr. SOMERS hints at. But after all, Sir, you do not indulge these apprehensions, on account of the general fickleness of human nature. You have some more particular reasons for concluding that the system of liberty, which hath worked such wonders of late, is not likely to maintain its ground amongst us.

MR. SOMERS.

I HAVE: and I was going to explain those reasons, if my lord of SALISBURY had not a little diverted me from the pursuit of them.

IT is very notorious from the common discourse of men even on this great occasion (and I wish it had not appeared too evidently in the debates of the houses), that

that very many of us have but crude notions of the form of government under which we live, and which hath been transmitted to us from our forefathers. I have met with persons of no mean rank, and supposed to be well seen in the history of the kingdom, who speak a very strange language. They allow, indeed, that something was to be done in the perilous circumstances into which we had fallen. But, when they come to explain themselves, it is in a way that leaves us no *right* to do any thing; at least, not what it was found expedient for the nation to do at this juncture. For they contend in so many words, " that the crown of *England is absolute*; that the form of government is an *entire and simple monarchy*; and that so it hath continued to be in every period of it down to the Abdication: that the CONQUEST, at least, to ascend no higher, invested the FIRST WILLIAM in absolute dominion; that from him it devolved of course

course upon his successors; and that all the pretended rights of the people, the GREAT CHARTERS of ancient and modern date, were mere usurpations on the prince, extorted from him by the necessity of his affairs, and revocable at his pleasure: nay, they insinuate that parliaments themselves were the creatures of his will; that their privileges were all derived from the sovereign's grant; and that they made no part in the original frame and texture of the *English* government.

IN support of this extraordinary system, they refer us to the constant tenor of our history. They speak of the Conqueror, as proprietary of the whole kingdom: which accordingly, they say, he parcelled out, as he saw fit, in grants to his *Norman* and *English* subjects: that, through his partial consideration of the church, and an excessive liberality to his favoured servants, this

distri-

distribution was so ill made, as to give occasion to all the broils and contentions that followed: that the church-men began their unnatural claim of independency on the crown; in which attempt they were soon followed by the encroaching and too powerful barons: that, in these struggles, many flowers of the crown were rudely torn from it, till a sort of truce was made, and the rebellious humour somewhat composed, by the extorted articles of RUNNING-MEDE: that these confusions, however, were afterwards renewed, and even increased, by the contests of the two houses of YORK and LANCASTER: but that, upon the union of the roses in the person of HENRY VII, these commotions were finally appeased, and the crown restored to its antient dignity and lustre: that, indeed the usage of parliaments, with some other forms of popular administration, which had been permitted in the former irregular reigns, was continued;

but

but of the mere grace of the prince, and without any confequence to his prerogative: that fucceeding kings, and even HENRY himfelf, confidered themfelves as poffeffed of an imperial crown; and that, though they might fometimes condefcend to take the advice, they were abfolutely above the control, of the people: in fhort, that the law itfelf was but the will of the prince, declared in parliament; or rather folemnly received and attefted there, for the better information and more entire obedience of the fubject.

THIS they deliver as a juft and fair account of the *Englifh* government; the genius of which, they fay, is abfolute and defpotic in the higheft degree; as much fo, at leaft, as that of any other monarch in *Europe*. They afk, with an air of infult, what reftraint our HENRY VIII, and our admired ELIZABETH, would ever fuffer to be put on their prerogative; and they mention
with

with derision the fancy of dating the high pretensions of the crown from the accession of the STUART family. They affirm, that JAMES I, and his son, aimed only to continue the government on the footing on which they had received it; that their notions of it were authorized by constant fact; by the evidence of our histories; by the language of parliaments; by the concurrent sense of every order of men amongst us: and that what followed in the middle of this century was the mere effect of POPULAR, as many former disorders had been of PATRICIAN, violence. In a word, they conclude with saying, that the old government revived again at the RESTORATION, just as, in like circumstances, it had done before at the UNION of the two houses: that, in truth, the voluntary desertion of the late king had given a colour to the innovation of the present year; but that, till this new settlement was made, the *English* constitution, as implying something different

ferent from pure monarchy, was an unintelligible notion, or rather a mere whimfy, that had not the leaſt foundation in truth or hiſtory."

This is a ſummary of the doctrines, which I doubt, are too current amongſt us. I do not ſpeak of the bigoted adherents to the late king; but of many cooler and more difintereſted men, whoſe *religious* principles, as I ſuppoſe (for it appears it could not be their *political*), had engaged them to concur in the new ſettlement. You will judge, then, if there be not reaſon to apprehend much miſchief from the prevalence and propagation of ſuch a ſyſtem: a ſyſtem, which, as being, in the language of the patrons of it, founded upon *fact*, is the more likely to impoſe upon the people; and, as referring to the practice of antient times, is not for every man's confutation. I repeat it, therefore; if this notion of the deſpotic form of our government become general,

general, I tremble to think what effect it may hereafter produce on the minds of men; especially when joined to that false tenderness, which the people of *England* are so apt to entertain for their princes, even the worst of them, under misfortune. I might further observe, that this prerogative-system hath a direct tendency to produce, as well as heighten, this compassion to the sovereign. And I make no scruple to lay it before you with all its circumstances, because I know to whom I speak, and that I could not have wished for a better opportunity of hearing it confuted.

BP. BURNET.

I must own, though I was somewhat unwilling to give way to such melancholy apprehensions at this time, I think with Mr. Somers, there is but too much reason to entertain them. For my own part, I am apt to look no further for the

right

right of the legiflature to fettle the government in their own way, than their own free votes and refolutions. For, being ufed to confider all political power as coming originally from the people, it feems to me but fitting that they fhould difpofe of that power for their own ufe, in what hands, and under what conditions, they pleafe. Yet, as much regard is due to eftablifhed forms and antient prefcription, I think the matter of *fact* of great confequence; and, if the people in general fhould once conceive of it according to this reprefentation, I fhould be very anxious for the iffue of fo dangerous an opinion. I muft needs, therefore, join very entirely with Mr. SOMERS, in wifhing to hear the whole fubject canvaffed, or rather finally determined, as it muft be if Sir JOHN MAYNARD will do us the pleafure to acquaint us what his fentiments are upon it.

SIR

SIR J. MAYNARD.

TRULY, my good friends, you have opened a very notable cause, and in good form. Only, methinks, a little less solemnity, if you had so pleased, might have better suited the occasion. Why, I could almost laugh, to hear you talk of fears and dangers from a phantom of your own raising. I certainly believe the common proverb belies us; and that old age is not that dastardly thing it hath been represented. For, instead of being terrified by this conceit of a prescriptive right in our sovereigns to tyrannize over the subject, I am ready to think the contrary so evident from the constant course of our history, that the simplest of the people are in no hazard of falling into the delusion. I should rather have apprehended mischief from other quarters; from the influence of certain speculative points, which have been too successfully propagated of late; and chiefly from those pernicious glosses, which too many of my order have made on the letter of the law, and too many of yours, my lord of SALISBURY, on that of the gospel. Trust me, if the matter once come to a question of FACT, and the inquiry be only concerning antient form and precedent, the decision will clearly be in our favour. And for yourselves, I assure myself, this decision is already made. But since you are willing to put me upon the task, and we have leisure enough for such an amusement, I shall very readily undertake it. And the rather, as I have more than once in my life had occasion to go to the bottom of this inquiry; and now very lately have taken a pleasure to reflect on the general evidence which history affords of our free constitution, and to review the scattered hints and passages I had formerly set down for my private satisfaction.

" I UNDERSTAND the question to be, not under what *form* the government
hath

hath appeared at some particular conjunctures, but what we may conclude it to have been from the general current and tenor of our histories. More particularly, I conceive, you would ask, not whether the *administration* hath not at some seasons been DESPOTIC, but whether the *genius* of the government hath not at all times been FREE. Or, if you do not think the terms, in which I propose the question, strict enough, you will do well to state it in your own way, that hereafter we may have no dispute about it.

BP. BURNET.

I SUPPOSE, the question, as here put, is determinate enough for our purpose. —Or, have you, Mr. SOMERS, any exceptions to make to it?

MR. SOMERS.

I BELIEVE we understand each other perfectly well; the question being only this,

this, "Whether there be any ground in history, to conclude that the prince hath a conftitutional claim to abfolute uncontrolable dominion; or, whether the liberty of the fubject be not effential to every different form, under which the *Englifh* government hath appeared?"

SIR J. MAYNARD.

You expect of me then to fhew, in oppofition to the fcheme juft now delivered by you, that neither from the original conftitution of the government, nor from the various forms (for they have, indeed, been various) under which it hath been adminiftered, is there any reafon to infer, that the *Englifh* monarchy is, or of right ought to be, defpotic and unlimited.

Now this I take to be the eafieft of all undertakings; fo very eafy, that I could truft a plain man to determine the matter for himfelf by the light that offers itfelf itself to him from the slightest of our histories. 'Tis true, the deeper his researches go, his conviction will be the clearer; as any one may see by dipping into my friend NAT. BACON's discourses; where our free constitution is set forth with that evidence, as must for ever have silenced the patrons of the other side, if he had not allowed himself to strain some things beyond what the truth, or indeed his cause, required. But, saving to myself the benefit of his elaborate work, I think it sufficient to take notice, that the system of liberty is supported even by that short sketch of our history, which Mr. SOMERS hath laid before us; and in spite of the disguises, with which, as he tells us, the enemies of liberty have endeavoured to cloak it.

You do not, I am sure, expect from me, that I should go back to the elder and more remote parts of our history;

that I should take upon me to investigate the scheme of government, which hath prevailed in this kingdom from the time that the *Roman* power departed from us; or that I should even lay myself out in delineating, as many have done, the plan of the *Saxon* constitution: though such an attempt might not be unpleasing, nor altogether without its use, as the *principles* of the *Saxon* policy, and in some respects the *form* of it, have been constantly kept up in every succeeding period of the *English* monarchy. I content myself with observing, that the spirit of liberty was predominant in those times: and, for proof of it, appeal at present only to one single circumstance, which you will think remarkable. Our *Saxon* ancestors conceived so little of government, by the will of the magistrate, without fixed laws, that LAGA, or LEAGA, which in their language first and properly signified the same as LAW with us,

was

was transferred [g] very naturally (for language always conforms itself to the genius, temper, and manners of a nation) to signify a country, district, or province; these good people having no notion of any inhabited country not governed by laws. Thus DÆNA-LAGA; MERKENA-LAGA;

[g] This casual remark seems to determine a famous dispute among the Antiquarians on the subject before us. Bishop NICHOLSON attended so little to this tralatitious use of words, in which all languages abound, that finding LAGA in several places signified a *country*, he would needs have it that CAMDEN, LAMBARD, SPELMAN, COWELL, SELDEN, and all our best Antiquaries, were mistaken, when they supposed *Laga* ever signified, in the compositions here mentioned, a *law*. However, his adversaries among the Antiquarians were even with him; and finding that *Laga*, in these compositions, did signify a law in several places of our ancient laws, historians, and lawyers, deny that it ever signifies a *country*. Each indeed had a considerable object in view; the one was bent on overthrowing a system; the other on supporting it; namely, that famous threefold body of laws, the *Danish, Mercian,* and *West-Saxon*. It must be owned, the bishop could not overthrow the common system, without running into his extreme: it seems, his opponents might have supported it, without running into theirs.

and WESTSEXENA-LAGA, were not only used in their laws and hiftory to fignify the *laws* of the *Danes*, *Mercians*, and *Weft-Saxons*, but the *countries* likewife. Of which ufage I could produce to you many inftances, if I did not prefume that, for fo fmall a matter as this, my mere word might be taken.

You fee then how fully the fpirit of liberty poffeffed the very language of our *Saxon* forefathers. And it might well do fo: for it was of the effence of the *German* conftitutions; a juft notion of which (fo uniform was the genius of the brave people that planned them) may be gathered, you know, from what the *Roman* hiftorians; and, above all, from what TACITUS hath recorded of them.

BUT I forbear fo common a topic: and, befides, I think myfelf acquitted of this tafk, by the prudent method, which the defenders of the regal power have
themfelves

themselves taken in conducting this controversy. For, as conscious of the testimony which the *Saxon* times are ready to bear against them, they are wise enough to lay the foundation of their system in the CONQUEST. They look no higher than that event for the origin of the *constitution*, and think they have a notable advantage over us in deducing their notion of the *English* government from the form it took in the hands of the *Norman* invader. But is it not pleasant to hear these men calumniate the improvements that have been made from time to time in the plan of our civil constitution with the name of *usurpations*, when they are not ashamed to erect the *constitution* itself on what *they* must esteem, at least, a great and manifest usurpation?

BP. BURNET.

CONQUEST, I suppose, in their opinion, gives *right*. And since an inquiry into the origin of a constitution requires
that

that we fix *somewhere*, confidering the vaſt alterations introduced by the Conqueſt, and that we have never pretended to reject, but only to improve and complete, the duke of NORMANDY's eſtabliſhment; I believe it may be as proper to ſet out from that æra as from any other.

SIR J. MAYNARD.

YOUR lordſhip does not imagine that I am about to excuſe myſelf from cloſing with them, even on their own terms. I intended that queſtion only as a reproach to the perſons we have to deal with; who, when a ſuccefsful event makes, or but ſeems to make, for their idol of an abſolute monarchy, call it a regular eſtabliſhment: whereas a revolution brought about by the juſteſt means, if the cauſe of liberty receive an advantage by it, ſhall be reviled by the name of uſurpation. But let them employ what names they pleaſe, provided their facts be well grounded.

grounded. We will allow them to dignify the *Norman* settlement with the title of CONSTITUTION. What follows? That *despotism* was of the essence of that constitution? So they tell us indeed; but without one word of proof, for the assertion. For what! do they think the name of conquest, or even the *thing*, implies an absolute unlimited dominion? Have they forgotten that WILLIAM's claim to the crown was, not *conquest* (though it enabled him to support his claim), but *testamentary succession:* a title very much in the taste of that time [*b*], and extremely reverenced by our *Saxon* ancestors? That, even waving this specious claim, he condescended to accept the crown, as a free gift; and by his coronation-oath submitted himself to the same terms of administration, as his predecessors? And that, in one word, he confirmed the *Saxon* laws, at least before

---

[*b*] See *Historical Law-Tracts,* vol. i. p. 294.

he

he had been many years in poſſeſſion of his new dignity [i]?

Is there any thing in all this that favours the notion of his erecting himſelf, by the ſole virtue of his victory at *Haſtings*, into an abſolute lord of the conquered country? Is it not certain that he bound himſelf, as far as oaths and declarations could bind him, to govern according to law; that he could neither touch the honours nor eſtates of his ſubjects but by legal trial; and that even the many forfeitures in his reign are an evidence of his proceeding in that method?

STILL we are told "of his parcelling out the whole land, upon his own terms, to his followers;" and are inſulted "with

[i] MILTON did not forget to obſerve, in his *Tenure of kings and magiſtrates*, That WILLIAM the *Norman*, though a Conqueror, and not unſworn at his Coronation, was compelled a ſecond time to take oath at *St. Albans*, ere the people would be brought to yield obedience." Vol. i. *of his Proſe works*, 4ᵗᵒ, 1753, p. 345.

his famous inftitution of feudal tenures." But what if the *former* of thefe affertions be foreign to the purpofe at leaft, if not falfe; and the *latter* fubverfive of the very fyftem it is brought to eftablifh? I think, I have reafon for putting both thefe queftions. For, what if he parcelled out moft, or all, of the lands of *England* to his followers? The fact has been much difputed. But be it, as they pretend, that the property of all the foil in the kingdom had changed hands: What is that to us, who claim under our *Norman*, as well as *Saxon*, anceftors? For the queftion, you fee, is about the form of government fettled in this nation at the time of the Conqueft. And they argue with us, from a fuppofed act of tyranny in the Conqueror, in order to come at that fettlement. The *Saxons*, methinks, might be injured, oppreffed, enflaved; and yet the conftitution, tranfmitted to us through his own *Normans*, be perfectly free.

BUT

But their *other* allegation is still more unfortunate. " He instituted, they say, the feudal law." True. But the feudal law, and absolute dominion, are two things; and, what is more, perfectly incompatible.

I take upon me to say, that I shall make out this point in the clearest manner. In the mean time, it may help us to understand the nature of the feudal establishment, to consider the practice of succeeding times. What that was, our adversaries themselves, if you please, shall inform us. Mr. Somers hath told their story very fairly; which yet amounts only to this, " That, throughout the *Norman* and *Plantagenet* lines, there was one perpetual contest between the prince and his feudataries for law and liberty:" an evident proof of the light in which our forefathers regarded the *Norman* constitution. In the competition of the

two

two ROSES, and perhaps before, they loſt ſight indeed of this prize. But no ſooner was the public tranquillity reſtored, and the contending claims united in HENRY VII, than the old ſpirit revived. A legal conſtitution became the conſtant object of the people; and, though not always avowed, was, in effect, as conſtantly ſubmitted to by the ſovereign.

IT may be true, perhaps, that the ability of *one* prince [k], the imperious carriage of *another* [l], and the generous intrigues of a *third* [m]; but above all, the condition of the times, and a ſenſe of former miſeries, kept down the ſpirit of liberty for ſome reigns, or diminiſhed, at leaſt, the force and vigour of its operations. But a paſſive ſubjection was never acknowledged, certainly never demanded as matter of right, till ELIZABETH now and then, and King JAMES, by talking

[k] HENRY VII.   [l] HENRY VIII.
[m] ELIZABETH.

continually

continually in this strain, awakened the national jealousy; which proved so uneasy to himself, and, in the end, so fatal to his family.

I CANNOT allow myself to mention these things more in detail to you, who have so perfect a knowledge of them. One thing only I insist upon, that, without connecting the system of liberty with that of prerogative in our notion of the *English* government, the tenor of our history is perfectly unintelligible; and that no consistent account can be given of it, but on the supposition of a LEGAL LIMITED CONSTITUTION.

MR. SOMERS.

YET that constitution, it will be thought, was at least ill defined, which could give occasion to so many fierce disputes, and those carried on through so long a tract of time, between the crown and the subject.

SIR J. MAYNARD.

THE fault, if there was one, lay in the original plan of the conſtitution itſelf; as you will clearly ſee when I have opened the nature of it, that is, when I have explained the genius, views, and conſequences of the FEUDAL POLICY. It muſt, however, be affirmed, that this policy was founded in the principles of freedom, and was, in truth, excellently adapted to an active, fierce, and military people; ſuch as were all thoſe to whom theſe weſtern parts of *Europe* have been indebted for their civil conſtitutions. But betwixt the burdenſome ſervices impoſed on the ſubject by this tenure, or which it gave at leaſt the pretence of exacting from him, and the too great reſtraint which an unequal and diſproportioned allotment of feuds to the greater barons laid on the ſovereign; but above all, by narrowing the plan of liberty too much; and, while it ſeemed

to

to provide for the dependency of the prince on one part of his subjects, by leaving both him and them in a condition to exercise an arbitrary dominion over all others: hence it came to pass that the feudal policy naturally produced the struggles and convulsions, you spoke of, till it was seen in the end to be altogether unsuited to the circumstances of a rich, civilized, and commercial people. The event was, that the inconveniences, perceived in this form of government, gradually made way for the introduction of a better; which was not, however, so properly a new form, as the old one amended and set right; cleared of its mischiefs and inconsistencies, but conducted on the same principles as the former, and pursuing the same end, though by different methods.

It is commonly said, "That the feudal tenures were introduced at the Conquest." But how are we to understand this assertion?

tion? Certainly, not as if the whole fyſtem of military ſervices had been created by the Conqueror; for they were eſſential to all the *Gothic* or *German* conſtitutions. We may ſuppoſe then, that they were only new modelled by this great prince. And who can doubt that the form, which was now given to them, would be copied from that which the *Norman* had ſeen eſtabliſhed in his own country? It would be copied then from the proper FEUDAL FORM; the eſſence of which conſiſted in the perpetuity of the feud [n]; whereas theſe military tenures had been elſewhere temporary only, or revocable at the will of the lord.

But to enter fully into the idea of the feudal conſtitution; to ſee at what time, and in what manner, it was introduced: above all, to comprehend the rea-

[n] PROPRIA FEUDI NATURA EST UT SIT PERPETUA. CUJACIUS, LITTLETON.

fons that occafioned this great change; it will be convenient to look back to the eftate of *France*, and efpecially of *Normandy*, where this conftitution had, for fome years, taken place before it was transferred to us at the Conqueft.

UNDER the firft princes of the *Carlovingian* line, the lands of *France* were of two kinds, ALLODIAL, and BENEFICIARY. The allodial, were eftates of inheritance; the perfons poffeffing them, were called HOMMES LIBRES. The beneficiary, were held by grants from the crown. The perfons holding immediately under the emperor, were called LEUDES; the fub-tenants, VASSALS.

FURTHER, the allodial lands were alienable, as well as hereditary. The beneficiary were properly neither. They were held for life, or a term of years, at the will of the lord, and reverted to him

on

on the expiration of the term for which they were granted.

I do not stay to explain thefe inftitutions minutely. It is of more importance to fee the alterations that were afterwards made in them. And the FIRST will be thought a ftrange one.

THE poffeffors of allodial lands, in *France*, were defirous to have them changed into *tenures*. They who held of the crown *in capite* were entitled to fome diftinctions and privileges, which the allodial lords wifhed to obtain; and therefore many of them furrendered their lands to the emperor, and received them again of him, in the way of *tenure*. This practice had taken place occafionally from the earlieft times: but under CHARLES the Bald, it became almoft general; and *free-men* not only chofe to hold of the emperor, but of other lords. This laft was firft allowed, in confequence of of a treaty between the three brothers, after the battle of *Fontenay* in 847.

But these *free-men* were not so ill advised as to make their estates precarious, or to accept a life-estate instead of an inheritance. It was requisite they should hold for a perpetuity. And this I take to have been the true origin of hereditary feuds. Most probably, in those dangerous times, little people could not be safe without a lord to protect them: and the price of this protection was the change of propriety into tenure.

The second change was by a law made under the same emperor in the year 877, the last of his reign. It was then enacted, that beneficiary estates held under the crown should descend to the sons of the present possessors: yet not, as I conceive, to the eldest son; but to him whom the emperor should chuse: nor did this law affect the estates only, but

but *offices*, which had hitherto been also beneficiary; and so the sons of counts, marquises, &c. (which were all names of offices, not titles of honour) were to succeed to the authority of their fathers, and to the benefice annexed to it. The new feuds, created in allodial lands, had, I suppose, made the emperor's tenants desirous of holding on the same terms: and the weakness of the reigning prince enabled them to succeed in this first step, which prepared the way for a revolution of still more importance. For,

THE THIRD change, by which the inheritance of beneficiary lands and offices was extended to perpetuity, and the possession rendered almost independent of the crown, was not, we may be sure, effected at once, but by degrees. The family of CHARLEMAGNE lost the empire: they resisted with great difficulty the incursions of the *Normans*; and in the year 911, *Normandy* was granted to
them

them as an hereditary fee. The great lords' made their advantage of the public calamities; they defended the king on what terms they pleafed; if not complied with in their demands, they refufed their affiftance in the moft critical conjunctures: and before the acceffion of Hugh Capet, had entirely fhaken off their dependence on the crown. For it is, I think, a vulgar miftake to fay, that this great revolution was the effect of Hugh's policy. On the contrary, the independence of the nobles, already acquired, was, as it feems to me, the caufe of his fuccefs. The prince had no authority left, but over his own demefnes; which were lefs confiderable than the poffeffions of fome of his nobles. Hugh had one of the largeft fiefs: and for this reafon, his ufurpation added to the power of the crown, inftead of leffening it, as is commonly imagined. But to bring back the feuds of the other nobles to their former precarious condition was

was a thing impossible: his authority was partly supported by superior wisdom, and partly by superior strength, his vassals being more numerous than those of any other lord.

I CANNOT tell if these foreigners, when they adopted the feudal plan, were immediately aware of all the consequences of it. An hereditary tenure was doubtless, a prodigious acquisition; yet the advantage was something counter-balanced by the great number of impositions which the nature of the change brought with it. These impositions are what, in respect of the lord, are called his FRUITS of tenure; such as WARDSHIP, MARRIAGE, RELIEF, and other services: and were the necessary consequence of the king's parting with his arbitrary disposal of these tenures. For now that the right of inheritance was in the tenant, it seemed but reasonable, and, without this provision, the feudal policy could not have obtained its end, that the prince, in these several ways, should secure to himself the honour, safety, and defence, which the very nature of the constitution implied and intended. Hence hereditary feuds were very reasonably clogged with the obligations I have mentioned; which, though trifling in comparison with the disadvantages of a precarious tenure, were yet at least some check on the independency acquired. However, these services, which were due to the king under the new model, were also due to the tenant in chief from those who held of him by the like tenure. And so the barons, or great proprietaries of land, considering more perhaps the subjection of their own vassals, than that by which themselves were bound to their sovereign, reckoned these burdens as nothing, with respect to what they had gained by an hereditary succession.

THE

The example of these *French* feudataries, we may suppose, would be catching. We accordingly find it followed, in due time, in *Germany*; where Conrad II [o] granted the like privilege of *successive* tenures, and at the pressing instance of his tenants.

I thought it material to remind you of these things; because they prove the feudal institution on the continent to have been favourable to the cause of liberty; and because it will abate our wonder to find it so readily accepted and submitted to here in *England*.

MR. SOMERS.

The account you have given, and, I dare say, very truly, of the origin of feuds in *France* and *Germany*, is such as shews them to have been an extension of the people's liberty. There is no question that hereditary alienable estates

[o] Craig's *Jus feudale*, lib. i. p. 21. *Lond.* 1655.

have

have vaſtly the preference to beneficiary. But the caſe, I ſuſpect, was different with us in *England*. The great offices of ſtate, indeed, in this country, as well as in *France*, were beneficiary. But, if I do not miſtake, the lands of the *Engliſh*, except only the church-lands, were all allodial. And I cannot think it could be for the benefit of the *Engliſh* to change their old *Saxon* poſſeſſions, ſubject only to the famous triple obligation, for theſe new and burdenſome tenures.

SIR J. MAYNARD.

STRANGE as it may appear, we have yet ſeen that the *French* did not ſcruple to make that exchange even of their allodial eſtates. But to be fair, there was a great difference, as you well obſerve, in the circumſtances of the two people. All the lands in *England* were, I believe, allodial, in the *Saxon* times: while a very conſiderable proportion of thoſe in *France* were beneficiary.

ANOTHER

Another difference, also, in the state of the two countries, is worth observing. In *France*, the allodial lands (though considerable in quantity) were divided into small portions. In *England*, they seem to have been in few hands; the greater part possessed by the King and his *Thanes*; some smaller parcels by the lesser *Thanes*; and a very little by the *Ceorles*. The consequence was, that, though the allodial proprietors in *France* were glad to renounce their property for tenure, in order to secure the protection they much wanted; yet with us, as you say, there could not be any such inducement for the innovation. For, the lands being possessed in large portions by the nobility and gentry, the allodial lords in *England* were too great to stand in need of protection. Yet from this very circumstance, fairly attended to, we shall see that the introduction of the feudal tenures was neither difficult nor unpopular.

lar. The great proprietors of land were, indeed, too free and powerful, to be bettered by this change. But their tenants, that is, the bulk of the people, would be gainers by it. For these tenants were, I believe, to a man beneficiaries. The large estates of the *Thanes* were granted out in small portions to others, either for certain quantities of corn or rent, reserved to the lord, or on condition of stipulated services. And these grants, of whichever sort they were, were either at pleasure, or at most for a limited term. So that, though the proprietors of land in *England* were so much superior to those in *France*; yet the tenants of each were much in the same state; that is, they possessed beneficiary lands on stipulated conditions.

When, therefore, by right of forfeiture, the greater part of the lands in *England* fell, as they of course would do, into the power of the king (for they were

were in few hands, and thofe few had either fought at *Haftings*, or afterwards rebelled againft him) it is eafy to fee that the people would not be difpleafed to find themfelves, inftead of beneficiary tenants [*p*], feudatary proprietors.

I say this on fuppofition that thefe great forfeited eftates and figniories, fo bountifully beftowed by the Conqueror on his favourite *Normans*, were afterwards, many of them at leaft, granted out in fmaller parcels to *Englifh* fub-tenants. But if thefe fub-tenants were alfo *Normans* (though the cafe of the *Englifh* or old *Saxon* freeholders was then very hard), the change of allodial into feudatary eftates is the more eafily accounted for.

[*p*] This account of the *Saxon* benefices is much confirmed by the famous charter of Bifhop Oswald, and the comment of Sir H. Spelman upon it. See his difcourfe on Feuds and Tenures.

The main difficulty would be with the churchmen; who (though the greatest, and most of them were, perhaps, *Normans* too) were well acquainted with the *Saxon* laws, and for special reasons were much devoted to them. They were sensible that their possessions had been held, in the *Saxon* times, in FRANC-ALMOIGN: a sort of tenure, they were not forward to give up for this of *feuds*. 'Tis true, the burdens of these tenures would, many of them, not affect them. But then neither could they reap the principal fruit of them, the fruit of inheritance. They, besides, considered every restraint on their privileges as impious; and took the subjection of the ecclesiastic to the secular power, which the feudal establishment was to introduce, for the vilest of all servitudes. Hence the churchmen were, of all others, the most averse from this law [*q*]. And their

[*q*] MATTHEW PARIS gives us the following account of this matter—" Episcopatus et Abbatias omnes,

their opposition might have given the conqueror still more trouble, if the suppression of the great northern rebellion had not furnished him with the power, and (as many of them had been deeply engaged in it) with the pretence, to force it upon them. And thus, in the end, it prevailed universally, and without exception.

I would not go further into the history of these tenures. It may appear from the little I have said of them, that the feudal system was rather improved and corrected by the duke of NORMANDY, than originally planted by him in this

omnes, quæ baronias tenebant, et eatenus ab omni servitute sæculari libertatem habuerant, sub servitute statuit militari, inrotulans singulos episcopatus et abbatias pro voluntate suâ, quot milites sibi et successoribus suis, hostilitatis tempore, voluit à singulis exhiberi. Et ROTULOS HUJUS ECCLESIASTICÆ SERVITUTIS ponens in thesauris, multos viros ecclesiasticos HUIC CONSTITUTIONI PESSIMÆ reluctantes, a regno fugavit."
     HIST. ANG. WILLIELMUS CONQUÆSTOR.

kingdom:

kingdom: that the alteration made in it was favourable to the public interest; and that our *Saxon* liberties were not so properly restrained, as extended by it. It is of little moment to inquire whether the nation was won, or forced, to a compliance with this system. It is enough to say, that, as it was accepted by the nation, so it was in itself no servile establishment, but essentially founded in the principles of liberty. The duties of lord and feudatary were reciprocal and acknowledged: services on the one part, and protection on the other. The institution was plainly calculated for the joint-interest [r] of both parties, and the benefit of the community; the proper

---

[r] The learned CRAIG, who has written so largely and accurately on the feudal law, was so far from seeing any thing servile in it, that he says, "The foundations of this discipline are laid in the most generous of all considerations, those of GRATITUDE. *Hujus feudalis disciplinæ fundamenta à gratitudine et ingratitudine descendunt.*" EPIST. NUNCUP. to K. JAMES.

ration

notion of the feudal fyftem being that "of a confederacy between a number of military perfons, agreeing on a certain limited fubordination and dependence on their chief, for the more effectual defence of his and their lives, territories, and poffeffions."

MR. SOMERS,

I HAVE nothing to object to your account of the feudal conftitution. And I think you do perfectly right, to lay the main ftrefs on the general nature and genius of it; as by this means you cut off thofe fruitlefs altercations, which have been raifed, concerning the perfonal character of the *Norman* Conqueror. Our concern is not with him, but with the government he eftablifhed. And if that be free, no matter whether the founder of it were a tyrant. But, though I approve your method, I doubt there is fome defect in your argument. *Freedom* is a term of much latitude. The *Norman* conftitution may be free in one fenfe, sense, as it excludes the sole arbitrary dominion of one man; and yet servile enough in another, as it leaves the government in few hands. For it follows, from what I understand of the feudal plan, that though its genius be indeed averse from absolute monarchy, yet it is indulgent enough to absolute *aristocracy*. And the notion of each is equally remote from what we conceive of true *English* liberty.

SIR J. MAYNARD.

It is true, the proper feudal form, especially as established in this kingdom, was in a high degree oligarchical. It would not otherwise, perhaps, have suited to the condition of those military ages. Yet the principles it went upon, were those of public liberty, and generous enough to give room for the extension of the system itself, when a change of circumstances should require it.—But your objection will best be answered by

looking

looking a little more distinctly into the nature of these tenures.

I took notice that the feudal system subjected the CHURCH more immediately to the civil power: and laid the foundation of many services and fruits of tenure to which the LAY-FEUDATARIES in the *Saxon* times had been altogether strangers. It is probable that all the consequences of this alteration were not foreseen. Yet the churchmen were pretty quick-sighted. And the dislike, they had conceived of the new establishment, was the occasion of those struggles, which continued so long between the mitre and crown, and which are so famous more especially in the early parts of our history. The cause of these ecclesiastics was a bad one. For their aim was, as is rightly observed by the advocates for the prerogative, to assert an independency on the state; and for that purpose the pope was made a party in the dispute;

dispute; by whose intrigues it was kept up in one shape or other till the total renunciation of the papal power. Thus far, however, the feudal constitution cannot be blamed. On the contrary, it was highly serviceable to the cause of liberty, as tending only to hold the ecclesiastic, in a due subordination to the civil, authority.

THE same thing cannot be said of the other instance, I mean the *fruits of tenure*, to which the lay-fees were subjected by this system. For however reasonable, or rather necessary, those *fruits* might be, in a feudal sense, and for the end to which the feudal establishment was directed, yet, as the *measure* of these fruits, as well as the manner of exacting them, was in a good degree arbitrary, and too much left to the discretion of the sovereign, the practice, in this respect, was soon found by the tenants in chief to be an intolerable grievance. Hence that other

other contest, so memorable in our history, betwixt the king and his barons: in which the former, under the colour of maintaining his feudal rights, laboured to usurp an absolute dominion over the persons and properties of his vassals; and the latter, impatient of the feudal burdens, or rather of the king's arbitrary exactions under pretence of them, endeavoured to redeem themselves from so manifest an oppression.

It is not to be denied, that, in the heat of this contest, the barons sometimes carried their pretensions still further, and laboured in their turn to usurp on the crown, in revenge for the oppressions they had felt from it. However, their first contentions were only for a mitigation of the feudal system. It was not the character of the *Norman* princes to come easily into any project that was likely to give the least check to their pretensions. Yet the grievances, complained of, of, were in part removed, in part moderated, by HENRY the firft's and many other fucceffive charters: though the laft blow was not given to thefe feudal fervitudes till after the Reftoration, when fuch of them as remained, and were found prejudicial to the liberty of the fubject, were finally abolifhed.

THUS we fee that one effential defect in the feudal policy, confidered not as a military, but civil inftitution, was, the too great power it gave the fovereign in the arbitrary impofitions, implied in this tenure. ANOTHER was accidental. It arofe from the difproportionate allotment of thofe feuds, which gave the greater barons an afcendant over the prince, and was equally unfavourable to the caufe of liberty. For the bounty of the duke of NORMANDY, in his diftribution of the forfeited eftates and figniories to his principal officers, had been fo
immenfe,

immense [s], that their share of influence in the state was excessive, and intrenched too much on the independency of the crown and the freedom of the people. And this undue poize in the constitution, as well as the tyranny of our kings, occasioned the long continuance of those civil wars, which for many ages harassed and distressed the nation. The evil, however, in the end, brought on its own remedy. For these princely houses being much weakened in the course of the quarrel, HENRY VII succeeded, at length, to the peaceable possession of the crown. And by the policy of this prince, and that of his successor, the barons were

[s] This bounty in so wise a prince as WILLIAM will be thought strange. I believe it may be, in part, accounted for, from what is observed above of the *Saxon* allodial lords. These had possessed immense estates. And, as they fell in upon forfeiture, the great *Norman* adventurers would of course expect to come into the entire succession.—Perhaps too, in that confusion of affairs, the prince might not always, himself, be apprized of the extent and value of these possessions.

brought

brought so low as to be quite disabled from giving any disturbance to the crown for the future.

It appears then that TWO great defects in the feudal plan of government, as settled amongst us, were, at length, taken away. But a THIRD, and the greatest defect of all, was the narrowness of the plan itself, I mean when considered as a system of CIVIL polity; for, in its primary martial intention, it was perfectly unexceptionable.

To explain this matter, which is of the highest importance, and will furnish a direct answer to Mr. SOMERS' objection, we are to remember that in the old feudal policy the king's barons, that is, such as held *in capite* of the crown by barony or knight's service, were the king's, or rather the kingdom's, great council. No public concerns could be regularly transacted, without their consent;

sent [*t*]; though the lesser barons, or tenants by knight's service, did not indeed so constantly appear in the king's court, as the greater barons; and though the public business was sometimes even left to the ordinary attendants on the king, most of them churchmen. It appears that, towards the end of the Conqueror's reign, the number of these tenants in chief was about 700; who, as the whole property of the kingdom was, in effect, in their power, may be thought a no unfit representative (though this be no proper *feudal* idea) of the whole nation. It was so, perhaps, in those rude and warlike times, when the strength of the nation lay entirely in the soldiery; that is, in those who held by military services, either immediately of the crown, or of the mesne lords. For the remainder of the people, whom

[*t*] The law of ELWARD the Confessor is express to this purpose, and it was ratified by the Conqueror—" Debet rex omnia ritè facere in regno et per judicium procerum regni." Sir H. SPELMAN of Parliaments, p. 58.

they

they called tenants in focage, were of small account; being confidered only in the light of fervants, and contributing no otherwife to the national fupport than by their cultivation of the foil, which left their mafters at leifure to attend with lefs diftraction on their military fervices. At leaft, it was perfectly in the genius of the feudal, that is, military conftitutions,' to have little regard for any but the men of arms; and, as every other occupation would of courfe be accounted bafe and ignoble, it is not to be wondered that fuch a difference was made between the condition of *prædial* and *military* tenures.

However, a policy, that excluded fuch numbers from the rank and privileges of citizens, was fo far a defective one. And this defect would become more fenfible every day, in proportion to the growth of arts, the augmentation of commerce, and the fecurity the nation found itfelf in from foreign dangers.'

The

The ancient military eftablifhment would now be thought unjuft, when the exclufive privileges of the fwordfmen were no longer fupported by the neceffities of the public, and when the wealth of the nation made fo great a part of the force of it. Hence arofe an important change in the legiflature of the kingdom, which was much enlarged beyond its former limits. But this was done gradually; and was more properly an extenfion than violation of the ancient fyftem.

First, The number of tenants in chief, or the king's freeholders, was much increafed by various caufes, but chiefly by the alienation which the greater barons made of their fees. Such alienation, though under fome reftraint, feems to have been generally permitted in the *Norman* feuds; I mean, till Magna Charta and fome fubfequent ftatutes laid it under particular limitations. But, whether the practice were regular or not,

not, it certainly prevailed from the earliest times; especially on some more extraordinary occasions. Thus, when the fashionable madness of the CROISADES had involved the greater barons in immense debts, in order to discharge the expences of these expeditions, they alienated their fees, and even dismembered them; that is, they parted with their right in them, and made them over in small parcels to others, to hold of the superior lord. And what these barons did from necessity, the crown itself did, out of policy: for the *Norman* princes, growing sensible of the inconvenience of making their vassals too great, disposed of such estates of their barons as fell into them by forfeiture, and were not a few, in the same manner. The consequence of all this was, that, in process of time, the lesser military tenants *in capite* multiplied exceedingly. And, as many of them were poor, and unequal to a personal attendance in the court of their lord,

lord, or in the common council of the kingdom (where of right and duty they were to pay their attendance) they were willing, and it was found convenient to give them leave, to appear in the way of *reprefentation*. And this was the origin of what we now call THE KNIGHTS OF THE SHIRES; who, in thofe times, were appointed to reprefent, not all the freeholders of counties, but the leffer tenants of the crown only. For thefe, not attending in perfon, would otherwife have had no place in the king's council.

THE rife of CITIZENS AND BURGESSES, that is, reprefentatives of the cities and trading towns, muft be accounted for fomewhat differently. Thefe had originally been in the jurifdiction, and made part of the demefnes, of the king and his great lords. The reafon of which appears from what I obferved of the genius of the feudal policy. For, little account being had of any but martial

tial men, and trade being not only difhonourable, but almoſt unknown in thoſe ages; the lower people, who lived together in towns, moſt of them ſmall and inconſiderable, were left in a ſtate of ſubjection to the crown, or ſome other of the barons, and expoſed to their arbitrary impoſitions and talliages.

But this condition of burghers, as it ſprang from the military genius of the nation, could only be ſupported by it. When that declined therefore, and, inſtead of a people of ſoldiers, the commercial ſpirit prevailed, and filled our towns with rich traders and merchants, it was no longer reaſonable, nor was it the intereſt of the crown, that theſe communities and bodies of men ſhould be ſo little regarded. On the contrary, a large ſhare of the public burdens being laid upon them, and the frequent neceſſities of the crown, eſpecially in foreign wars, or in the king's contentions with his barons,

barons, requiring him to have recourse to their purses, it was naturally brought about that those, as well as the tenants *in capite*, should, in time, be admitted to have a share in the public councils.

I do not stay to trace the steps of this change. It is enough to say, that it arose insensibly and naturally out of the growing wealth and consequence of the trading towns; the convenience the king found in drawing considerable sums from them, with greater ease to himself, and less offence to the people; and, perhaps, from the view of lessening by their means, the exorbitant power and influence of the barons.

From these, or the like reasons, the great towns and cities, that before were royal demesnes, part of the king's private patrimony, and talliable by him at pleasure, were allowed to appear in his council by their deputies, to treat with him

him of the proportion of taxes to be raised on them, and, in a word, to be considered in the same light as the other members of that great assembly.

I DO not inquire when this great alteration was first made. I find it subsisting at least under EDWARD III. And from that time, there is no dispute but that the legislature, which was originally composed of the sovereign and his feudal tenants, included also the representatives of the counties, and of the royal towns and cities. To speak in our modern style, the HOUSE OF COMMONS was, now, formed. And by this addition, the glorious edifice of *English* liberty was completed.

I AM sensible, I must have wearied you with this deduction, which can be no secret to either of you. But it was of importance to shew, that the constitution of *England*, as laid in the feudal tenures,
was

was essentially free; and that the very changes it hath undergone, were the natural and almost unavoidable effects of those tenures. So that what the adversaries of liberty object to us, as usurpations on the regal prerogative, are now seen to be either the proper result of the feudal establishment, or the most just and necessary amendments of it.

BP. BURNET.

I HAVE waited with much pleasure for this conclusion, which entirely discredits the notion of an absolute, despotic government. I will not take upon me to answer for Mr. SOMERS, whose great knowledge in the laws and history of the kingdom enables him to see further into the subject than I do; but to me nothing appears more natural or probable than this account of the rise and progress of the *English* monarchy. One difficulty, in particular, which seemed to embarrass this inquiry, you have entirely removed, by shewing how, from the aristocratical form which prevailed in the earlier times, the more free and popular one of our days hath gradually taken place, and that without any violence to the antient constitution [*u*].

MR. SOMERS.

At least, my lord, with so little, that we may, perhaps, apply to the *English* government what the naturalists observe of the HUMAN BODY [*w*]; that, when it arrives at its full growth, it does not perhaps retain a single particle of the matter it originally set out with; yet the

[*u*] M. DE MONTESQUIEU observes of the Gothic government—"Il fut d'abord mêlé de l'aristocra-"tie, et de la monarchie. Il avoit cet inconvenient, "que le bas-peuple y étoit esclave: C'étoit un bon "gouvernment, qui avoit en soi la capacité de devenir "meilleur." [l. xi. c. 8.]—the very idea, which is here inculcated.

[*w*] See old FORTESCUE, in his book *De laudibus legum Angliæ*, where this sort of analogy is pursued at length through a great part of the xiiith chapter.

alteration

alteration hath been made so gradually and imperceptibly, that the system is accounted the same under all changes. Just so, I think, we seem to have shaken off the constituent parts of the FEUDAL CONSTITUTION; but, liberty having been always the informing principle, time and experience have rather completed the old system, than created a new one: and we may account the present and *Norman* establishment all one, by the same rule as we say that HERCULES, when he became the deliverer of oppressed nations, was still the same with him who had strangled serpents in his cradle.

SIR J. MAYNARD.

I KNOW not what fanciful smiles your younger wit may delight in. I content myself with observing, that the two great points, which they, who deny the liberty of the subject, love to inculcate, and on which the plausibility of all their reasonings depends, are, THE SLAVISH NATURE

OF THE FEUDAL CONSTITUTION, and THE LATE RISE OF THE HOUSE OF COMMONS. And I have taken up your time to small purpose, if it doth not now appear, that the *former* of these notions is false, and the *latter* impertinent. If the learned inquirers into this subject had considered that the question is concerning the freedom itself of our constitution, and not the most convenient form under which it may be administered, they must have seen that the feudal law, though it narrowed the system of liberty, was founded in it; that the spirit of freedom is as vital in this form, and the principles it goes upon as solid, as in the best-formed republic; and that *villanage* concludes no more against the *feudal* than *slavery* against the *Greek* or *Roman*, constitutions.

MR. SOMERS.

THAT is, Sir JOHN, you make *liberty* to have been the essence of all THREE; though,

though to the perfection of an equal commonwealth, you suppose it should have been further spread out and dilated: as they say of *frankincense* (if you can forgive another allusion), which, when lying in the lump, is of no great use or pleasure; but, when properly diffused, is the sweetest of all odours. But you was going on with the application of your principles.'

SIR J. MAYNARD.

I was going to say that, as many have been misled by wrong notions of the *feudal tenures*, others had erred as widely in their reasonings on *the late origin of the lower house of parliament*. How have we heard some men triumph, in dating it no higher than the reign of EDWARD III? Let the fact be admitted. What follows? That this house is an usurpation on the prerogative? Nothing less. It was gradually brought forth by time, and grew up under the favour and good liking of our princes [*x*]. The constitution itself supposed the men of greatest consequence in the commonwealth to have a seat in the national councils. Trade and agriculture had advanced vast numbers into consequence, that before were of small account in the kingdom. The public consideration was increased by their wealth, and the public necessities relieved by it. Were these to remain for ever excluded from the king's councils? or was not that council, which had liberty for its object, to widen and expand itself in order to receive them? It did, in fact, receive them with open arms; and, in so doing, conducted itself on the very principles of the old feudal policy.

[*x*] Agreeably to what Sir H. SPELMAN asserts, in his Glossary, of its parent, the *feudal law* itself; " DE LEGE FEUDALI—pronunciandum censeo, TEMPORIS eam esse filiam, sensimque succrescentem, EDICTIS PRINCIPUM auctam indies et excultam.' In voce FEODUM.

In short, the *feudal constitution*, different from all others that human policy is acquainted with, was of such a make, that it readily gave way, and fitted itself to the varying situations of society: narrow and contracted, when the public interest required a close connexion between the governor and the governed; large and capacious, when the same interest required that connexion to be loosened. Just as the skin (if you will needs have a comparison), the natural cincture of the body, confines the young limbs with sufficient tightness, and yet widens in proportion to their growth, so as to let the different parts of the body play with ease, and obtain their full size and dimensions. Whereas the other policies, that have obtained in the world, may be compared to those artificial coverings, which, being calculated only for one age and size, grow troublesome and insupportable in any other; and yet cannot, like these, be be thrown off and supplied by such as are more suitable and convenient; but are worn for life, though with constant, or rather increasing, uneasiness.

This then being the peculiar prerogative of the feudal policy, I think we may say with great truth, not that the house of commons violated the constitution, but, on the contrary, that the constitution itself demanded, or rather generated, the house of commons.

So that I cannot by any means commend the zeal which some have shewn in seeking the origin of this house in the *British* or even *Saxon* annals. Their aim was, to serve the cause of liberty; but, it must be owned at the expence of truth, and, as we now perceive, without the least necessity.

BP. BURNET.

It hath happened then in this, as in so many other instances, that an excellent cause

cause hath suffered by the ill judgment of its defenders. But, when truth itself had been disgraced by one sort of men in being employed by them to the worst purposes, is it to be wondered that others should not acknowledge her in such hands, but be willing to look out for her in better company?

SIR J. MAYNARD.

Let us say, my lord, they should have acknowledged her in whatever company she was found; and the rather, as ill-applied truths are seen to be full as serviceable to a bad cause, as downright falsehoods. Besides, this conduct had not only been fairer, but more politic. For when so manifest a truth was rejected, it was but natural to suspect foul play in the rest, and that none but a bad cause could want to be supported by so disingenuous a management.

MR.

MR. SOMERS.

I THINK so, Sir JOHN; and there is this further use of such candor, that it cuts off at once the necessity of long and laboured researches into the dark parts of our history; and so not only shortens the debate, but renders it much more intelligible to the people.

SIR J. MAYNARD.

I WAS aware of that advantage, and am therefore not displeased that truth allowed me to make use of it.—But to resume the main argument; for I have not yet done with my evidence for the freedom of our excellent constitution:—It seemed of moment to shew, from the nature and consequences of the *Norman* settlement, that the *English* government was essentially free. But, because the freest form of government may be tamely given up and surrendered into the hands of a master, I hold it of consequence

quence to prove, that the *English* spirit hath always been anſwerable to the conſtitution, and that even the moſt inſidious attempts on their liberties have never failed to awaken the reſentment of our generous forefathers. In a word, I would ſhew that the jealouſy, with which the *English* have ever guarded the national freedom, is at once a convincing teſtimony of their *right*, and of their conſtant *poſſeſſion* of it.

AND though I might illuſtrate this argument by many other inſtances, I chuſe to inſiſt only on ONE, THEIR PERPETUAL OPPOSITION TO THE CIVIL AND CANON LAWS; which, at various times and for their ſeveral ends, the crown and church have been ſolicitous to obtrude on the people.

To open the way to this illuſtration, let it be obſerved that, from the time of HONORIUS, that is, when the *Roman* authority

thority ceased amongst us, the *Saxon* institutions, incorporated with the old *British* customs, were the only standing laws of the kingdom. These had been collected and formed into a sort of digest by EDWARD the Confessor; and so great was the nation's attachment to them, that WILLIAM himself was obliged to ratify them, at the same time that the feudal law itself was enacted. And afterwards, on any attempt to innovate on those laws, we hear of a general outcry and dissatisfaction among the people: which jealousy of theirs, was not without good grounds; as we may see from an affair that happened in the Conqueror's own reign, and serves to illustrate the policy of this monarch.

IT had been an old custom, continued through the *Saxon* times, for the bishops and sheriffs to sit together in judicature in the county courts. This had been found a very convenient practice; for
the

the presence of the churchmen gave a sanction to the determinations of the temporal courts, and drew an extraordinary reverence towards them from the people. Yet we find it abolished by the Conqueror; who, in a rescript to the bishop of *Lincoln*, ordained that, for the future, the bishops and aldermen of the shires should have separate courts and separate jurisdictions. The pretence for this alteration was, the distinct nature of the two judicatures, and the desire of maintaining a strict conformity to the canons of the church. The real design was much deeper. There is no question but WILLIAM's inclinations, at least, were for arbitrary government; in which project his *Norman* lawyers, it was hoped, might be of good use to him. But there was a great obstacle in his way. The church men of those times had incomparably the best knowledge of the *Saxon* laws. It matters not, whether those churchmen were *Normans*, or not. They were equally

equally devoted, as I observed before, to the *Saxon* laws, with the *English*; as favouring that independency, they affected, on the civil power. Besides, in the Confessor's time, many and perhaps the greatest of the churchmen had been *Normans*; so that the study of the *Saxon* laws, from the interest they promised themselves in them, was grown familiar to the rising ecclesiastics of that country. Hence, as I said, the churchmen, though *Normans*, were well instructed in the spirit and genius of the *Saxon* laws; and it was not easy for the king's glossers to interpret them to their own mind, whilst the bishops were at hand to refute and rectify their comments.

Besides, the truth is (and my lord of Salisbury will not be displeased with me for telling it), the ecclesiastics of that time were much indevoted to the court. They considered the king as the wickedest of all tyrants. He had brought them
into

into subjection by their baronies, and had even set the pope himself at defiance. In this state of things, there was no hope of engaging the clergy in his plot. But, when a separation of the two tribunals was made, and the civil courts were solely administered by his own creatures, the laws, it was thought, would speak what language he pleased to require of them.

SUCH appears to have been the design of this prince in his famous distinction of the ecclesiastic and temporal courts. It was so artfully laid and so well coloured, that the laity seem to have taken no umbrage at it. But the clergy saw his drift; and their zeal for the antient laws, as well as their resentments, put them upon contriving methods to counteract it. They hit upon a very natural and effectual one. In a word, they all turned common lawyers; and so found means of introducing themselves into the civil courts.

courts. This expedient succeeded so well, and was so generally relished, that the clergy to a man almost in the next reign were become professors of the common law; NULLUS CLERICUS NISI CAUSIDICUS, as WILLIAM of *Malmesbury* takes care to inform us [*y*].

BP. BURNET.

WHATEVER their motive might be, the churchmen, I perceive, interposed very seasonably in the support of our civil liberties. It was a generous kind of revenge, methinks, to repay the king's tyranny over the church by vindicating the authority of the *English* laws.

SIR J. MAYNARD.

IT was so; and for this good service, I let them pass without any harsher reflection. Though the true secret is, perhaps, no more than this: Their main

[*y*] DISS. AD FLET. 1091. and WILLIAM OF MALMESBURY, lib. iv. f. 69. *Lond.* 1596.

object

object was the church, of whose interests, as is fitting, we will allow them to be the most competent judges. And, as these inclined them, they have been, at different junctures, the defenders or oppressors of civil liberty.

BP. BURNET.

AT *some* junctures, it may be, they have. But, if you insist on so general a censure, I must intreat Mr. SOMERS, once more, to take upon him the defence of our order.

SIR J. MAYNARD.

ALL I intended by this instance, was, to shew the spirit of the *Saxon* laws, which could excite the jealousy of the prince, and deserve, at such a season, the patronage of the clergy. It seems, however, for once, as if they had a little misconceived their true interests. For the distinction of the two judicatures, which occasioned their resentment, was, in the end, a great means of the hierarchical greatness and independency.

MATTERS continued on this footing during the three firſt of the *Norman* reigns. The prince did his utmoſt to elude the authority of the *Engliſh* laws; and the nation, on the other hand, laboured hard to confirm it. But a new ſcene was opened under King STEPHEN, by means of the *Juſtinian* laws; which had lately been recovered in *Italy*, and became at once the faſhionable ſtudy over all *Europe*. It is certain, that the Pandects were firſt brought amongſt us in that reign; and that the reading of them was much favoured by Archbiſhop THEOBALD [z], under whoſe encouragement they were publicly read in *England* by VACARIUS, within a ſhort time after the famous IRNERIUS had opened his ſchool at *Bologna*. There is ſomething ſingular in the readineſs with

[z] SELDEN's Works, vol. ii. p. 1082.

which

which this new fyftem of law was embraced in thefe weftern parts of *Europe*. But my friend Mr. SELDEN ufed to give a plaufible account of it. It was, he faid [a], in oppofition to INNOCENT II, who was for obtruding on the Chriftian ftates the *decretals*, as laws; manifeftly calculated for the deftruction of the civil magiftrate's power. And what feems to authorize the opinion of my learned friend, is, that the popes very early took the alarm, and, by their decrees, forbad churchmen to teach the civil law: as appears from the conftitution of ALEXANDER III, fo early as the year 1163, in the council of TOURS; and afterwards from the famous decretal of SUPER-SPECULA by HONORIUS III, in 1219, in which the clergy of all denominations, feculars as well as regulars, were prohibited the ftudy of it. And it was, doubtlefs, to defeat the mifchief which the popes apprehended to themfelves,

[a] DISS. AD FLET. 1078.

selves, from the credit of the imperial laws, that GRATIAN was encouraged, about the same time, to compose and publish his DECREE; which, it is even said [b], had the express approbation of pope EUGENIUS.

LET us see, now, what reception this newly-recovered law, so severely dealt with by the pope, and so well entertained by the greatest part of *Europe*, had in *England*.

VACARIUS had continued to teach it for some time, in the archbishop's palace at *Lambeth*, to great numbers, whom first, the novelty of the study, and then, the fashion of the age, had drawn about him. The fame of the teacher was high, and the new science had made a great progress, when on a sudden it received a severe check, and from a quarter

[b] DR. DUCK, *De usu et authoritate juris civilis*, p. 103. *Lugd. Batav.* 1654.

whence

whence one should not naturally expect it. In short, the king himself interdicted the study of it. Some have imagined, that this inhibition was owing to the spite he bore to archbishop THEOBALD. But the truer reason seems to be, that the canon law was first read by VACARIUS at the same time, and under colour of the imperial. I think we may collect thus much very clearly from JOHN OF SALISBURY, who acquaints us with this edict. For he considers it as an offence against the church, and expressly calls the prohibition, an IMPIETY [c].

IT is true, the decretals of GRATIAN were not yet published. But Ivo had made a collection of them in the reign of HENRY I; and we may be sure that some code of this sort would privately go about amongst the clergy, from what was before observed of the pains taken

[c] POLICRATIC. lib. viii. c. 22. p. 672. *Lugd Bat.* 1639.

by INNOCENT II, to propagate the decretals. We may further obferve, that THEOBALD had been in high favour with INNOCENT; and that his fchool, at *Lambeth,* was opened immediately on his return from *Rome,* whither he had been to receive his pall from this pope, on his appointment to the fee of *Canterbury* [d]. All which makes it probable, that STEPHEN's difpleafure was not fo much at the civil, as *canon* law, which he might well conclude had no friendly afpect on his fovereignty.

AND we have the greater reafon to believe that this was the fact, from obferving what afterwards happened in the reign of HENRY III, when a prohibition of the fame nature was again iffued out againft the teachers of the *Roman* laws in *London* [e]. The true caufe of the royal mandate is well known. GREGORY IX

[d] DISS. AD FLET. 1082. [e] Ibid. 1097.

had

had juft then publifhed a new code of the decretals; which, like all former collections of this fort, was calculated to ferve the papal intereft, and deprefs the rights of princes.

However, thefe edicts, if we fuppofe them levelled againft the civil law, had no effect, any more than thofe of the popes Alexander and Honorius, before mentioned. For the imperial law, being generally well received by the princes of *Europe*, prefently became a kind of *Jus gentium*. And the clergy, who afpired to power and dignities, either abroad or at home, ftudied it with an inconceivable rage; infomuch, that Roger Bacon tells us, that, in his time for forty years together, the feculars, who were the ecclefiaftics employed in bufinefs, never publifhed a fingle treatife in divinity [*f*].

[*f*] Dr. Duck, p. 364.

THE truth is, whatever shew the popes or our own princes might make, at times, of discountenancing the civil law, it was not the design of either absolutely and universally to suppress it. It was properly, not the civil, but the canon law, which was discountenanced by our kings. And the case of the popes was, that, when they found the imperial law opposed to the *common*, they were ready to favour it; when it was opposed to the *canon*, and brought that into neglect, they forbad ecclesiastics the study of it.

MR. SOMERS.

IN the mean time the poor people, methinks, were in a fine condition, between two laws, the one founded on civil, and the other on ecclesiastical, tyranny. If either had prevailed, there had been an end of their liberties.

SIR J. MAYNARD.

CERTAINLY their situation was very critical. Yet in the end it was precisely this situation that saved them. For betwixt these contentions of the crown and mitre, each endeavouring to extend its dominion over the other, the people, who were of course to be gained by either side in its distress, found means to preserve themselves from both.

To see how this happened, we must remember, what appears indeed from the two edicts of STEPHEN and HENRY, that the king himself was a bulwark betwixt them and the papal power. And when the king in his turn wanted to exalt his prerogative over all, the church very naturally took the alarm, as we saw in the case of WILLIAM's separation of the two tribunals. And thus it happened, as NAT. BACON observes [g], "That

[g] DISC. Part I. p. 78. *Lond.* 1739.

many times the pope and the clergy became protectors of the people's liberties, and kept them safe from the rage of kings. The greatest danger was, when the two powers chanced to unite in one common defign againſt them; as they did in their general inclination for the eſtabliſhment of the civil law. But here the people had the courage always to defend themſelves; and with that wiſdom too, as demonſtrates their attention to the cauſe of civil liberty, and the vigilance with which they guarded even its remoteſt outworks.

Of their ſteady and watchful conduct, in this reſpect, I ſhall mention ſome of the many memorable examples, that occur in our hiſtory.

I have ſaid that from the time of Stephen, notwithſtanding his famous edict, the imperial laws were the chief and favourite ſtudy of the clergy. They
had

had good reason for applying themselves so closely to this science, and still further views than their own immediate advancement. They wanted to bring those laws into the civil courts, and to make them the standing rule of public administration; not merely from their good-will to the papal authority, which would naturally gain an advantage by this change, but for the sake of controlling the too princely barons, and in hopes, no doubt, that the imperial would in due time draw the canon laws into vogue along with them. Such, I think, were at least the secret designs of the ruling clergy; and they did not wait long before they endeavoured to put their project in execution. The plot was admirably laid, and with that deep policy as hath kept it, I believe, from being generally understood to this day.

The great men of that time were, we may be sure, too like the great men of every

every other, to be very scrupulous about the commission of those vices to which they were most inclined. The truth is, their profligacy was in proportion to their greatness and their ignorance. They indulged themselves in the most licentious amours, and even prided themselves in this licence. The good churchmen, no doubt, lamented this corruption of manners; but, as they could not reform, they resolved at least to draw some emolument to themselves from it. The castles of the barons, they saw, were full of bastards. Nay, the courtesy of that time had so far dignified their vices, that the very name was had in honour. EGO GULIELMUS BASTARDUS, is even the preamble to one of WILLIAM the first's charters.

YET, as respectable as it was become, there was one unlucky check on this favourite indulgence: and this, with the barons leave, the considerate bishops
would

would presently take off. Subsequent marriage, by the imperial as well as canon laws, legitimated bastards, as to succession; whereas the common law kept them eternally in their state of bastardy. It is not to be doubted, but the barons would be sensible enough of this restraint. They earnestly wished to get rid of it. And could any thing bid so fair to recommend the imperial law to their good liking, as the tender of it for so desirable a purpose? At a parliament, therefore, under HENRY III [*b*], *Rogaverunt omnes episcopi, ut consentirent quod nati ante matrimonium essent legitimi.* What think ye now of this general supplication of the hierarchy? What could the barons do but comply with it, especially as it was so kindly intended for their relief, and the proposal was even made with a delicacy that might enable them to come into it with a good grace, and without the shame of seeming to

[*b*] At MERTON, in the year 1236.

desire it? All this is very true. Yet the answer of the virtuous barons is as follows: *Omnes comites et barones unâ voce responderunt,* QUOD NOLUMUS LEGES ANGLIÆ MUTARI.

WE see then what stuck with them. These barons, as licentious as they were, preferred their liberty to their pleasure. The bishops they knew, as partisans of the pope, were for subjecting the nation to the imperial and papal laws. They offered, indeed, to begin with a circumstance very much to their taste. But if they accepted the benefit of them in one instance, with what decency could they object to them in others? They determined therefore to be consistent. They rejected a proposition, most agreeable in itself, lest their acceptance of it should make way for the introduction of foreign laws; whose very genius and essence, they well knew, was arbitrary, despotic power. Their answer speaks their sense of this matter, NOLUMUS LEGES ANGLIÆ MUTARI. They had nothing to object to the proposal itself. But they were afraid for the constitution.

MR. SOMERS.

I DOUBT, Sir JOHN, my lord of SALISBURY will bring a fresh complaint against you, for this liberty with the bishops. But I, who shall not be thought wanting in a due honour for that bench, must needs confess myself much pleased, as well with the novelty, as justice of this comment. I have frequently considered this famous reply of the old barons. But I did not see to the bottom of the contrivance. Their aversion to the imperial laws, as you say, must have been very great, to have put them on their guard against so inviting a proposal.

BP. BURNET.

ONE thing, however, is forgotten or dissembled in this account, that the law of
JUSTINIAN,

JUSTINIAN, which allows the privilege of legitimation to subsequent marriage, is grounded on some reasons that might, perhaps, recommend it to the judgment, as well as interest of the old prelates. Besides, they doubtless found themselves much distressed by the contrariety of the two laws in this instance. For the ground of their motion, as I remember, was, *Quod esset secundum communem formam ecclesiæ.* But, to deal ingenuously with you, Sir JOHN, you have dressed up your hypothesis very plausibly. And I, who am no advocate for the civil or ecclesiastical laws, in this or any instance where they clash with those of my country, can allow your raillery on HENRY's good bishops, if it were only that I see it makes so much for your general argument.

SIR J. MAYNARD.

YOUR lordship may the rather excuse this liberty with the *church*, as I propose,

pose, in due time, to deal as freely with
WESTMINSTER-HALL; a similar plot,
which I shall have occasion to mention
presently, having been formed against
the antient constitution by the men of
our profession.

MR. SOMERS.

IN the mean time, Sir JOHN, you must
give me leave, in quality of advocate for
the church, to observe one thing, that
does the churchmen honour. It is, that,
in these attempts on the constitution, the
judges and great officers of the realm,
who in those times were of the clergy,
constantly took the side of the *English*
laws; as my Lord COKE himself, I remember, takes notice in his commentary
on this statute of MERTON.

SIR J. MAYNARD.

I BELIEVE the observation is very
just. But I should incline to impute this
integrity, not to the influence of church
principles,

principles, but thofe of the common law, and fo turn your compliment to the honour of our profeffion inftead of theirs, if it were not too clear in fact that every profeffion, in its turn, hath been liable to this charge of corruption.

But I was going on with my proofs of the national averfion to the imperial law.

The next fhall be taken from that famous difpute concerning the fucceffion to the crown of *Scotland* in the reign of Edward I. For a queftion arifing about the kind of law by which the controverfy fhould be decided, and it being efpecially debated, whether the *Cæfarean* law, as a fort of *jus gentium*, ought not, in fuch a caufe, to have the preference to the law of *England*; it was then unanimoufly determined by the great council of Norham, that the authority of the *Cæfarean* law fhould by no means
be

be admitted; NE INDE MAJESTATIS ANGLICANÆ JURI FIERET DETRIMENTUM [*i*].

THIS determination was public, and given on a very folemn occafion. And in general we may obferve, that at the junctures when the ftate hath been moft jealous of its liberty and honour, it hath declared the loudeft againft the *imperial laws:* as in the WONDER-WORKING parliament under RICHARD II, when the duke of *Gloucefter* accufed the archbifhop of *York*, the duke of *Ireland*, and other creatures of the king, of high treafon. The charge was fo fully proved, that the court had no other way of diverting the ftorm, than by pretending an irregularity in the forms of procedure. To this end the lawyers were confulted with, or more properly directed. I will difguife nothing. They defcended fo much from the dignity of

[*i*] DISS. AD FLET. 1108.

their profession, as to act in perfect subserviency to the views of the court; and therefore gave it as their opinion, that the proceedings against the lords were of no validity, as being contrary to the forms prescribed by the *civil law*. The barons took themselves to be insulted by these shifts of the lawyers. They insisted that the proceedings were agreeable to their own customs, and declared roundly that they would never suffer *England* to be governed by the *Roman* civil law [k].

WHAT think ye now of these examples? Are they not a proof that the spirit of liberty ran high in those times, when neither the intrigues of churchmen nor the chicane of lawyers could put a stop to it? It seems as if no direct attempts on the constitution could have

[k] See FORTESCUE, *De laudibus leg. Angl.* p. 74. *Lond.* 1741; and SELDEN's JANUS ANGLORUM, 1010, vol. ii. tom. ii.

been

been made with the least appearance of success; and that therefore the abettors of arbitrary power were obliged to work their way obliquely, by contriving methods for the introduction of a foreign law.

In this project they had many advantages, which nothing but an unwearied zeal in the cause of liberty could have possibly counteracted. From the reign of STEPHEN to that of EDWARD III, that is, for the space of near 200 years, the *Roman* law had been in great credit [l]. All the learning of the times was in the clergy, and that learning was little more than the imperial and canon laws. The fact is so certain, that some of the clergy themselves, when in an ill temper, or off their guard, complain of it in the strongest terms. And to see the height to which this humour was carried, not the seculars only who intend-

[l] Diss. ad Flet. 1104.

ed to rife by them, but the very monks in their cells ftudied nothing but thefe laws [*m*]. To complete the danger, the magiftracies and great offices of the kingdom were filled with churchmen [*n*].

WHO would expect, now, with thofe advantages, but that the *Roman* law would have forced its way into our civil courts? It did indeed infinuate itfelf there as it were by ftealth, but could never appear with any face of authority. The only fervice, that would be accepted from it, was that of illuftration only in the courfe of their pleadings, whilft the lawyers quoted occafionally from the INSTITUTES, juft as they might have done from any other ancient author [*o*]. Yet, fo long as the churchmen prefided in the courts of juftice, this intruder was to be refpected; and it is pleafant to ob-ferve the wire-drawing of fome of our

[*m*] Dr. DUCK, p. 365.
[*n*] DISS. AD FLET. 1010.   [*o*] Ibid. 1106.

ableft

ablest lawyers, in their endeavours to make the policy of *England* speak the language of *Rome*.

MR. SELDEN'S dissertation on FLETA [*p*], which lies open before me, affords a curious instance. The civil law says, " Populus ei [Cæsari] et in eum omne suum imperium et potestatem conferat;" meaning by *people*, the *Roman* people, and so establishing the despotic rule of the prince. But BRACTON took advantage of the ambiguity, to establish that maxim of a free government, " That all dominion arises from the people." This you will say, was good management. But what follows is still better. " Nihil aliud, says he, potest rex in terris, cum sit Dei minister et vicarius, nisi quod JURE potest. NEC OBSTAT quod dicitur, QUOD PRINCIPI PLACET LEGIS HABET VIGOREM; quia sequitur in fine legis, CUM LEGE REGIA QUÆ DE

[*p*] P. 1046.

IMPERIO EJUS LATA EST; id eft, non quicquid de voluntate regis temerè præfumptum eft, fed quod confilio magiftratuum fuorum, rege auctoritatem præftante, et habitâ fuper hoc deliberatione et tractatu, rectè fuerit definitum." Thus far old BRACTON; who is religioufly followed in the fame glofs by THORNTON, and the author of FLETA. But what! you will fay, this is an exact defcription of the prefent conftitution. It is fo, and therefore certainly not to be found in the civil law. To confefs the truth, thefe venerable fages are playing tricks with us. The whole is a premeditated falfification, or, to fay it fofter, a licentious commentary, for the fake of *Englifh* liberty. The words in the PANDECTS and INSTITUTIONS are thefe; "QUOD PRINCIPI PLACUIT, LEGIS HABET VIGOREM, UTPOTE CUM LEGE REGIA, QUÆ DE IMPERIO EJUS LATA EST, POPULUS EI ET IN EUM OMNE SUUM IMPERIUM ET POTESTATEM CONFERAT."

My

My honest friend, in mentioning this extraordinary circumstance, says, one cannot consider it, *sine stupore*. He observes, that these lawyers did not quote the Pandects by hear-say, but had copies of them; and therefore adds (for I will read on) " Unde magis mirandum quânam ratione evenerit, ut non solùm ipse, adeò judiciis forensibus clarus, et (si Biographis scriptorum nostratium fides) professor juris utriusque Oxoniensis, verùm etiam THORNTONIUS juris aliàs peritissimus, et FLETÆ author, adeò diversam lectionem, sensumque diversum atque interpretibus aliis universis adeò alienum in illustrissimo juris Cæsarei loco explicando tam fidentèr admiserint." The difficulty, you see, increases upon him. But we shall easily remove it by observing, that the Cæsarean laws, though they had no proper authority with us, yet were much complimented in those times, and were to be treated on all occasions with ceremony.

And

And therefore thofe lawyers that lived under and wanted to fupport a free conftitution, faw there was no way of ferving their caufe fo effectually, as by pretending to find it in the *Roman inftitutes.*

MR. SOMERS.

THIS management of BRACTON and his followers makes fome amends for the ill conduct of RICHARD the fecond's lawyers. And as to their chicanery, the ingenuity of the glofs, we will fuppofe, was no more than neceffary to correct the malignity of the text.

SIR J. MAYNARD.

THEY had, no doubt, confulted their honour much more, by infifting roundly, as they might have done, that the text had no concern at all in the difpute. But I mention thefe things only to fhew the extreme reverence, that was then paid to the civil law, by the fhifts the common lawyers were put to in order to evade

evade its influence. From which we learn how rooted the love of liberty muſt have been in this nation, and how unſhaken the firmneſs of the national councils in ſupporting it, when, notwithſtanding the general repute it was of in thoſe days, the imperial law could never gain authority enough to preſcribe to us in any matters that concerned the rights of the crown, or the property of the ſubject. And this circumſtance will be thought the more extraordinary, if it be conſidered, that, to the general eſteem in which the *Roman* law was held by the clergy, our kings have uſually added the whole weight of their influence; except indeed at ſome particular junctures, when their jealouſy of the *canon* law prevailed over their natural bias to the *civil.*

MR. SOMERS.

I should be unwilling to weaken any argument you take to be of uſe in maintaining the noble cauſe you have undertaken.

taken. But, methinks, this charge on our princes would require to be made out by other evidence [*q*] than hath been commonly produced for it. There is no doubt but many of them have aimed at setting themselves above the laws of their country; but is it true (I mean, though FORTESCUE himself [*r*] has suggested the same thing) that for this purpose they have usually expressed a partiality to the *Roman* laws?

SIR J. MAYNARD.

I BELIEVE it certain that they have, and on better reasons than the bare word of any lawyer whatsoever.

WHAT think you of RICHARD the second's policy in the instance before mentioned; that RICHARD, who used to declare, " That the laws were only in his mouth and breast, and that he himself

---

[*q*] Mr. SELDEN's DISS. AD FLET. 1109.
[*r*] *De laud. leg. Ang.* c. 33, 34.

could

could make and unmake them at his pleasure?" We may know for what reason a prince of this despotic turn had recourse to the *Roman* law.

But even his great predecessor is known to have been very indulgent towards it. And still earlier, EDWARD I. took much pains to establish the credit of this law; and to that end engaged the younger ACCURSIUS, the most renowned doctor of the age, to come over into *England*, and set up a school of it at *Oxford*. Or, to wave these instances, let me refer you to a certain and very remarkable fact, which speaks the sense, not of this or that king, but of the whole succession of our princes.

THE imperial law, to this day, obtains altogether in the courts of admiralty, in courts marescall, and in the universities [s]. On the contrary, in what we

[s] Diss. ad Flet. 1102.

call

call the courts of law and equity, it never hath, nor ever could prevail. What shall we say to this remarkable difference? or to what cause will you ascribe it, that this law, which was constantly excluded with such care from the one sort of courts, should have free currency and be of sole authority in the other? I believe it will be difficult to assign any other than this: that the subjects of decision in the first species of courts are matters in the resort of the king's prerogative, such as peace and war, and the distribution of honours; whilst the subjects of decision in the courts of common law are out of his prerogative, such as those of liberty and property. The king had his choice by what law the first sort of subjects should be regulated; and therefore he adopted the imperial law. He had not his choice in the latter instance; and the people were never satisfied with any other than the law of the land.

MR.

MR. SOMERS.

YET Mr. SELDEN, you know, gives another reason of this preference: it was, he thinks, because foreigners are often concerned with the natives in those tribunals where the civil law is in use.

SIR J. MAYNARD.

TRUE; but my learned friend, as I conceive, did not attend to this matter with his usual exactness. For foreigners are as frequently concerned in the courts of law and equity, as in the other tribunals. The case in point of reason is very clear. In all contests that are carried on between a native and a foreigner, as the subject of another state, the decision ought to be by the law of nations. But when a foreigner puts himself with a native under the protection of our state, the determination is, of course, by our law. The practice hath uniformly corresponded to the right in the courts of
law

law and equity. In the other tribunals the right hath given way to the will of the prince, who had his reasons for preferring the authority of the imperial law.

Upon the whole, if we consider the veneration, which the clergy usually entertained, and endeavoured to inculcate into the people, for the civil law; the indulgence shewn it by the prince; its prevalence in those courts which were immediately under the prerogative; and even the countenance shewn it at times in the course of pleading at common law; we cannot avoid coming to this short conclusion, "That the genius of the imperial laws was repugnant to our constitution; and that nothing but the extreme jealousy of the barons, lest they might prove, in pleas of the crown, injurious to civil liberty, hath kept them from being received in *England* on the same footing that we every where find

they

they are in the other countries of *Europe*, and as they are in *Scotland* to this day.

But, if you think I draw this conclusion too hastily, and without grounding it on sufficient premises, you may further consider with me, if you please, THE FATE AND FORTUNES OF THE CIVIL LAW IN THIS KINGDOM DOWN TO THE PRESENT TIME.

In the reigns of HENRY VII [*i*] and VIII, and the two first kings of the house of

[*i*] The speaker might have begun this account of the *fate and fortunes* of the civil law still higher. NAT. BACON, speaking of HENRY the fifth's reign, observes, " The times were now come about, wherein light began to spring forth, conscience to bestir itself, and men to study the scriptures. This was imputed to the idleness and carelessness of the clergy, who suffered the minds of young scholars to luxuriate into errors of divinity, for want of putting them on to other learning; and gave no encouragement to studies of human literature, by preferring those that were deserving. The convocation taking this into consideration, do decree, that no person should exercise any jurisdiction in any office, as

vicar-

of STUART, that is, the moſt deſpotic of our princes, the ſtudy of the civil law hath been more eſpecially favoured; as we might conclude from the general ſpirit of thoſe kings themſelves, but as we certainly know from the countenance they ſhewed to its profeſſors; from their chuſing to employ them in their buſineſs, and from the ſalaries and places they

vicar-general, commiſſary, or *official,* or otherwiſe, unleſs he ſhall firſt in the univerſity have taken degrees in the CIVIL or CANON LAWS. A ſhrewd trick this was, to ſtop the growth of the ſtudy of divinity, and WICKLIFF's way; and to embelliſh men's minds with a kind of learning that may gain them preferment, or at leaſt an opinion of abilities beyond the common ſtrain, and dangerous to be meddled with. Like ſome gallants, that wear ſwords as badges of honour, and to bid men beware, becauſe they poſſibly may ſtrike, though in their own perſons they may be very cowards. And no leſs miſchievouſly intended was this againſt the rugged COMMON LAW, a rule ſo nigh allied to the goſpel-way, as it favoureth liberty; and ſo far eſtranged from the way of the civil and canon law, as there is no hope of accommodation till Chriſt and Antichriſt have fought the field." Diſc. Part II. p. 90. *Lond.* 1739.

provided

provided for their encouragement. Yet see the iſſue of all this indulgence to a foreign law, and the treatment it met with from our parliaments and people! The oppreſſions of Empson and Dudley had been founded in a ſtretch of power, uſurped and juſtified on the principles of the civil law; by which theſe miſcreants had been enabled to violate a fundamental part of our conſtitution, the way of *trial by* juries. The effect on the people was dreadful. Accordingly, in the entrance of the next reign, though the authority, by which they had acted, had even been parliamentary, theſe creatures of tyranny were indicted of high treaſon, were condemned and executed for having been inſtrumental in ſubverting legem terræ; and the extorted ſtatute, under which they had hoped to ſhelter themſelves, was with a juſt indignation repealed.

YET all this was confidered only as a neceffary facrifice to the clamours of an incenfed people. The younger HENRY, we may be fure, had fo much of his father in him, or rather fo far outdid him in the worft parts of his tyranny, that he could not but look with an eye of favour on the very law he had been conftrained to abolifh. His great ecclefiaftical minifter was, no doubt, in the fecret of his mafter's inclinations, and conducted himfelf accordingly. Yet the vengeance of the nation purfued and overtook him in good time. They refented his difloyal contempt of the original conftitution; and made it one of the articles againft this *Roman* cardinal, " That he endeavoured to fubvert *antiquiffimas leges hujus regni, univerfumque hoc regnum* LEGIBUS IMPERIALIBUS *fubjicere.*"

FROM

FROM this time, the study of the civil law was thought to languish in *England*, till it revived with much spirit in the reigns of those unhappy princes who succeeded to the house of TUDOR. Then indeed, by inclination and by pedantry, JAMES I, was led to patronize and encourage it. And the same project was resumed, and carried still further, by his unfortunate son. I speak now from my own experience and observation. The civil lawyers were most welcome at court. They were brought into the Chancery and court of Requests. The minister, another sort of man than WOLSEY, yet a thorough ecclesiastic, and bigoted, if not to the religion, yet to the policy of *Rome*, gave a countenance to this profession above that of the common law. He had found the spirit, and even the forms of it, most convenient for his purpose in the STAR-CHAMBER and HIGH-COMMISSION court, those tribunals of imperial juſtice, exalted ſo far above the controul of the common law; and by his good will, therefore, he would have brought the ſame regimen into the other branches of the adminiſtration. Great civilians were employed to write elaborate defences of their ſcience; to the manifeſt exaltation of the prerogative; to the prejudice of the national rights and privileges; and to the diſparagement of the common law. The conſequence of theſe proceedings is well known. The moſt immediate was, that they provoked the jealouſy of the common lawyers; and, when the rupture afterwards happened, occaſioned many of the moſt eminent of them to throw themſelves into the popular ſcale [*u*].

YET, to ſee the uniformity of the views of tyranny, and the direct oppo-

[*u*] It ſhould however be obſerved, in honour of their patriotiſm, that " they afterwards took themſelves out of it," when they ſaw the extremities to which the popular party were driving.

ſition

fition which it never fails to encounter from the *English* law, no fooner had a fet of violent men ufurped the liberties of their country, and with the fword in their hands determined to rule defpotically and in defiance of the conftitution, than the fame jealoufy of the common law, and the fame contempt of it revived. Nay, to fuch an extreme was the new tyranny carried, that the very game of EMPSON and DUDLEY was played over again. The trial of an *Englifhman*, by his peers, was difgraced and rejected; and (I fpeak from what I felt) the perfon imprifoned and perfecuted, who dared appeal, though in his own cafe [w], to the

[w] This alludes to the proceedings againft the *eleven members* upon the charge of the army. Sir JOHN MAYNARD was one of them. And when articles of high treafon were preferred againft him, and the trial was to come on before the lords, he excepted to the jurifdiction of the court, and, by a written paper prefented to them, required to be tried by his peers according to *Magna Charta, and the law of the land*. See WHITLOCKE's *Memorials*;

the ancient essential forms of the constitution. Under such a state of things, it is not to be wondered that much pains was taken to depreciate a law which these mighty men were determined not to regard. Invectives against the professors of the *English* laws were the usual and favoured topics of parliamentary eloquence. These were sometimes so indecent, and pushed to that provoking length, that WHITLOCKE himself, who paced it with them through all changes, was forced in the end to hazard his reputation with his masters, by standing on the necessary defence of himself and his profession [x].

I NEED not, I suppose, descend lower. Ye have both seen with your own eyes and a short pamphlet written on that occasion, called THE ROYAL QUARREL, dated 9th of *Feb.* 1647.— Sir JOHN was, at this time, a close prisoner in the Tower.

[x]. See his speech, inserted in his *Memorials of English affairs,* Nov. 1649.

the

the occurrences of the late reign. Ye have heard the common language of the time. The practice was but conformable to such doctrines as were current at court, where it was generally maintained, that the king's power of dispensing with law, was LAW; by which if these doctors did not intend the *imperial* or *civil law*, the insult was almost too gross to deserve a confutation. It must be owned, and to the eternal shame of those who were capable of such baseness, there were not wanting some even of the common lawyers that joined in this insult.

I but touch these things slightly; for I consider to whom I speak. But if, to these examples of the nation's fondness for their laws, you add, what appears in the tenor of our histories, the constant language of the *coronation-oaths, of the oaths of our judges*, and, above all, of the *several great charters*; in all which express mention

is

is made of the LEX TERRÆ, in opposition to every foreign, but especially the Cæsarean, law; you will conclude with me, "That, as certainly as the CÆSAREAN LAW is founded in the principles of slavery, our ENGLISH LAW, and the constitution to which it refers, hath its foundation in freedom, and, as such, deserved the care with which it hath been transmitted down to us from the earliest ages."

WHAT think ye now, my good friends? Is it any longer a doubt, that the constitution of the *English* government, such I mean as it appears to have been from the most unquestioned annals of our country, is a free constitution? Is there any thing more in the way of this conclusion? or does it not force itself upon us, and lie open to the mind of every plain man that but turns his attention upon this subject?

You

You began, Mr. SOMERS, with great fears and apprehensions; or you thought fit to counterfeit them, at least. You suspected the matter was too mysterious for common understandings to penetrate, and too much involved in the darkness of ancient times to be brought into open daylight. Let me hear your free thoughts on the evidence I have here produced to you. And yet it is a small part only of that which might be produced, of that I am sure which yourself could easily have produced, and perhaps expected from me.

BUT I content myself with these obvious truths, " That the liberty of the subject appears, and of itself naturally arose, from the very nature of the FEUDAL, which is properly (at least if we look no further back than the Conquest) the *English* constitution; that the current of liberty has been gradually widening, as well

well as purifying, in proportion as it defcended from its fource; that charters and laws have removed every fcruple that might arife about the reciprocal rights and privileges of prince and people; that the fenfe of that liberty which the nation enjoyed under their admirable conftitution was fo quick, that every the leaft attempt to deprive them of it, gave an alarm; and their attachment to it fo ftrong and conftant, that no artifice, no intrigue, no perverfion of law and gofpel could induce them to part with it: that, in particular, they have guarded this precious depofite of legal and conftitutional liberty with fuch care, that, while the heedlefs reception of a foreign law, concurring with other circumftances, hath riveted the yoke of flavery on the other nations of *Europe*, this of *England* could never be cajoled nor driven into any terms of accommodation with it; but, as NAT. BACON [y] faid truly, *That the*

[y] DISC. Part I. p. 78.

triple

triple crown could never well folder with the English, so neither could the *imperial*; and that, in a word, the ENGLISH LAW hath always been preserved inviolate from the impure mixtures of the canon and Cæsarean laws, as the sole defence and bulwark of our civil liberties."

THESE are the plain truths, which I have here delivered to you, and on which I could be content to rest this great cause; I mean, if it had not already received its formal, and, I would hope, final determination, in another way. For no pretences will surely prevail hereafter with a happy people to renounce that liberty, which so rightfully belonged to them at all times, and hath now so solemnly been confirmed to them by the great transactions of these days. I willingly omit therefore, as superfluous, what in a worse cause might have been thought of no small weight, the express testimony of our ablest lawyers to
the

the freedom of our conſtitution. I do not mean only the COKES and SELDENS of our time (though in point of authority what names can be greater than theirs?); but thoſe of older and therefore more reverend eſtimation, ſuch as GLANVIL, BRACTON, the author of FLETA, THORN-TON, and FORTESCUE [z]: men the moſt eſteemed and learned in their ſeveral ages; who conſtantly and uniformly ſpeak of the *Engliſh*, as a mixed and limited

[z] The reader may not be diſpleaſed to ſee the words of old FORTESCUE on this ſubject of the origin of the *Engliſh* government, which are very remarkable. In his famous book *De laudibus legum Angliæ*, he diſtinguiſhes between the REGAL and POLITICAL forms of government. In explaining the *latter*, which he gives us as the proper form of the *Engliſh* government, he expreſſeth himſelf in theſe words—" Habes inſtituti omnis POLITICI REGNI formam, ex quâ metiri poteris poteſtatem, quam rex ejus in leges ipſius aut ſubditos valeat exercerę: ad tutelam namque legis ſubditorum, ac eorum corporum et bonorum rex hujuſmodi erectus eſt, et hanc poteſtatem A POPULO EFFLUXAM ipſe habet, quo ei non licet poteſtate aliâ *ſuo populo dominari*." CAP. xiii.

form

form of government, and even go so far as to seek its origin, where indeed the origin of all governments must be sought, in the free will and consent of the people.

All this I might have displayed at large; and to others perhaps, especially if the cause had required such management, all this I should have displayed. But, independently of the judgments of particular men, which prejudice might take occasion to object to, I hold it sufficient to have proved from surer grounds, from the very form and make of our political fabric, and the most unquestioned, because the most public, monuments of former times, " THAT THE ENGLISH CONSTITUTION IS ASSUREDLY AND INDISPUTABLY FREE [*a*]."

BP.

[*a*] It may be of little moment to us, at this day, to inquire, how far the princes of the house of STUART were blameable for their endeavours to usurp on the constitution. But it must ever be of the highest moment to maintain, that we had a constitution

BP. BURNET.

You will read, Sir JOHN, in our attention to this difcourfe, the effect it has had upon us. The zeal, with which you have pleaded the caufe of liberty, makes me almoft imagine I fee you again in the warmth and fpirit of your younger years, when you firft made head againft the encroachments of civil tyranny. The fame caufe has not only recalled to your memory the old topics of defence, but reftores your former vigour in the management of them. So that, for myfelf, I muft freely own, your vindication of our common liberties is, at leaft, the moft plaufible and confiftent that I have ever met with.

MR. SOMERS.

AND yet, if one was critically difpofed, there are ftill, perhaps, fome things that

ftitution to affert againft them. Party-writers perpetually confound thefe two things. It is the author's purpofe, in thefe two Dialogues, to contend for the *latter*.

might

might deserve a further explanation.—
But enough has been said by you, Sir
JOHN, to shew us where the truth lies:
and, indeed, from such plain and convincing topics, that, whatever fears my
love of liberty might suggest, they are
much abated at least, if not entirely removed, by your arguments.

BP. BURNET.

MR. SOMERS, I perceive, is not easily
cured of his scruples and apprehensions.
But for my own part, Sir JOHN, I can
think but of one objection of weight that
can be opposed to your conclusion. It
is, "That, notwithstanding the clear evidence you have produced, both for the
free nature of the *English* constitution,
and the general sense of the *English*
nation concerning it, yet, in fact, the government was very despotic under the
TUDOR, and still more perhaps under
the first princes of the STUART, line.
How could this happen, may it be asked,

on your plan, which fuppofes the popular intereft to have been kept up in conftant vigour, or rather to have been always gaining, infenfibly indeed, but neceffarily, on the power of the crown? Will not the argument then from hiftorical evidence be turned againft you, whilft it may be faid that your theory, however plaufible, is contradicted by fo recent and fo well-attefted a part of our hiftory? And, in particular, will not the partifans [b] of the late king and his family have to allege in their behalf, that their notions of the prerogative were but fuch as they fucceeded to with the crown; and, whatever may be pretended from refearches into remoter times, that they endeavoured only to maintain the monarchy on the footing on which it had ftood for many fucceffions, and on which it then ftood with the adminiftra-

[b] See the late Hiftory of England by DAVID HUME, Efq; who forms the apology of the houfe of STUART on thefe principles.

tion fell into their hands? If this point were effectually cleared, I see nothing that could be further desired to a full and complete vindication of *English* liberty.

SIR J. MAYNARD.

Your lordship, I must own, has touched a very curious and interesting part of our subject. But you must not believe it was so much overlooked by me, as purposely left for your lordship's better consideration. You, who have looked so minutely and carefully into the story of those times, will, better than any other, be able to unfold to us the mysteries of that affair. The fact is certain, as you say, that the *English* government wore a more despotic appearance from the time of the TUDOR family's accession to the throne, than in the reigns preceding that period. But I am mistaken, if your lordship will not open the reason of it so clearly as to convince us, that that increase of prerogative was no proof of a change in the conſtitution, and was even no ſymptom of declining liberty. I do not allow myſelf to ſpeak my ſentiments more plainly at preſent. But I am ſure, if they are juſt, they will receive a confirmation from what your lordſhip will find occaſion to obſerve to us in diſcourſing on this ſubject.

MR. SOMERS.

I will not diſown that this was one of the matters I had in view, when I hinted ſome remaining doubts about your general concluſion. But I knew it would not eſcape my lord of Salisbury, who, of all others, is certainly the moſt capable of removing it.

BP. BURNET.

So that I have very unwarily, it ſeems, been providing a fine taſk for myſelf. And yet, as difficult as I foreſee it will be for me to ſatisfy two ſuch Inquirers, I ſhould not decline that taſk, if I was indeed

deed prepared for it, or if I could boast of such a memory as Sir J. MAYNARD has shewn in the course of this conversation. But the truth is, though I have not wanted opportunities of laying in materials for such a design, and though I have not neglected to take some slight notes of them, yet I cannot pretend to have them at once in that readiness, as to venture on such a discourse as I know you expect from me. But if, against our next meeting, I shall be able to digest such thoughts as have sometimes occurred to me when I was engaged in the History of the Reformation, I shall take a pleasure to contribute all I can to the further and more entire elucidation of this subject.

And yet myself, ... I ... I could boast
of had a ... as Sir J. Middleton
has the ... e whole of this conversation ... been ... Laugh I have
nor ... appearance of being in
... such a design, and though
I have no ... to take some slight
notes of them, yet I cannot proceed to
have them at once in that readiness, as to
venture on such a utterance as I know
you ... them me. But if, against
our ... ations, I shall be able to obtain ... ... have sometimes
occurred to me when I was engaged in
the ... , ... the ... uation, I shall
take a pleasure in communicate all I can
to the ... , and so the same elucidation of this subject.

DIALOGUE VI.

On the CONSTITUTION of the ENGLISH Government.

SIR JOHN MAYNARD, MR. SOMERS, BISHOP BURNET.

TO DR. TILLOTSON.

OUR next meeting at Sir J. MAYNARD's was on the evening of that day, when the war was proclaimed againſt *France* [c]. What the event of it will be, is a ſecret in the counſels of Providence. But if the goodneſs of our cauſe, his majeſty's known wiſdom and ability, and above all the apparent zeal and firmneſs of all orders amongſt us in ſupport of this great undertaking, may

[c] 7 May, 1689.

give

give a prospect of success, we cannot, I persuade myself, but indulge in the most reasonable hopes and expectations.

PERHAPS, the time is approaching, my dear friend, which the divine goodness hath decreed for putting a stop to that outrageous power, which hath been permitted for so long a course of years to afflict the neighbouring nations. It may be, the season is now at hand, when God will vouchsafe to plead the cause of his servants, and let this mighty persecutor of the faithful know that he may not be suffered any longer to trample on the sacred rights of conscience. He may be taught to feel, that the ravages he hath committed in the fairest provinces, and the cruelties he hath exercised on the best subjects, of his own kingdom, have at length awakened the divine displeasure against him. And he may live to find in our great prince (raised up, as I verily believe, to this

eminence

eminence of place and power to be the scourge of tyrants, and the vindicator of oppressed nations) an insurmountable bulwark against that encroaching dominion, which threatens to deform and lay waste the rest of *Europe*.

I HAVE already lived to see those providences, which may encourage a serious and good mind to believe that some great work is preparing in our days. I was very early in my life a witness to the high measures which were taken and carried on by an intolerant hierarchy, acting in subserviency to an arbitrary court, in mine own country of *Scotland*. And I have lamented the oppression in which good men were held for conscience sake in all the three kingdoms. How far this tyranny was carried, and how near we were brought to the destruction of all our civil and religious rights, need not be told, and the occurrences of the two last reigns will not suffer to be forgotten.

gotten. It is sufficient to obferve, that when the danger was now brought to a crifis, and the minds of all men were filled with the moft alarming apprehenfions, it pleafed God to refcue us, in a moment, and by the moft aftonifhing difplay of his goodnefs, from the impending ruin. Our chains fell off at once, as by a miracle of mercy. Our civil rights have been reftored. And the legal toleration [*d*], we have juft now obtained in confequence of the new fettlement, hath put us into poffeffion of that religious liberty, which, as men, as Chriftians, and as Proteftants, we cannot but efteem the firft of all public bleffings.

AND who knows but that, in the gracious defigns of heaven, the fame hand which hath redeemed thefe nations from the yoke of flavery and of *Rome*, may be

---

[*d*] The act of toleration did not pafs till 24 *May*, 1689; which lets us fee at what time this preface is *fuppofed* to have been drawn up.

now

now employed to shake it off from the necks of our Proteſtant brethren on the continent [e]? The world hath ſeen how long and how ſeverely they have groaned under that intolerant power, with which we are now at war. When the violences of the late reign had driven me into a ſort of voluntary exile, and in the courſe of it I traverſed ſome of thoſe unhappy provinces of *France*, which were moſt expoſed to the rigours of perſecution [f], how have theſe eyes wept

[e] This was the talk of men at that time. It was perhaps in the king's intention. But the deſign, if it had ever been formed, miſcarried; as the Biſhop himſelf obſerves in his Hiſtory—" The moſt " melancholy part of the treaty of *Ryſwick* was, that " no advantages were got by it, in favour of the " Proteſtants in *France*." Vol. iv. p. 295. *Edinb.* 1753.—Whether the blame of this lies in the king, or his parliaments, or neither, the reader is left to judge for himſelf, from conſidering the ſtate and tranſactions of thoſe times.

[f] Theſe rigours the biſhop gives a particular account of in THE HISTORY OF HIS OWN TIMES, vol. iii. *Edinb.* 1753.—Speaking of the perſecution

of

wept over the diftreſſes of the poor ſufferers, and how hath my heart bled for the mercileſs cruelties which I every where ſaw exerciſed upon them! The fury which appeared on that occaſion, was ſo general and ſo contagious, that not only prieſts and court ſycophants, but men of virtuous minds and generous tempers were tranſported, as it were, out of their proper nature, and ſeemed to diveſt

of the *French* Proteſtants, he ſays, " I went over a
" great part of *France*, while it was in its hotteſt
" rage, from *Marſeilles* to *Montpelier*, and from
" thence to *Lyons*, and ſo on to *Geneva*. I ſaw and
" knew ſo many inſtances of their injuſtice and vio-
" lence, that it exceeded even what could have been
" well imagined; for all men ſet their thoughts
" on work to invent new methods of cruelty. In
" all the towns through which I paſſed, I heard the
" moſt diſmal accounts of things poſſible." p. 60.—
Again—" The fury that appeared on this occaſion
" did ſpread itſelf with a ſort of contagion: for the
" intendants and other officers, that had been mild
" and gentle in the former parts of their life, ſeemed
" now to have laid aſide the compaſſion of Chriſtians,
" the breeding of gentlemen, and the impreſſions of
" humanity." p. 61.

themſelves

themselves of the common notices and principles of humanity.

In this fiery trial it hath pleased God to exercise the faith and virtues, and, as we may charitably hope, to correct the failings and vices, of his poor servants. His mercy may now, in due time, be opening a way for them to escape. And from the prosperous beginning of this great work, what comfortable presages may we not, in all humility, form to ourselves of still further successes?

We have a prince on the throne exactly qualified for the execution of this noble enterprise; of the clearest courage and magnanimity, and a wisdom tried and perfected in that best school, of Adversity; of dispositions the most enlarged to the service of mankind; and even quickened by his own personal resentment of former injuries to retaliate against their common oppressor.

NOR can we doubt of the concurrence of his faithful subjects, who, with one voice, have demanded the commencement of this war; and whose late deliverance, from like circumstances of distress, may be expected to animate their zeal in the support of it.

AND oh! that I might see the day, when our deliverer shall become, what a bold usurper nobly figured to himself in the middle of this century [g], the soul and conductor of the Protestant cause through all *Europe!* and, that, as *Rome* hath hitherto been the centre of slavish impositions and anti-christian politics, the court of *England* may henceforth be the constant refuge and asylum of fainting liberty and religion!

[g] Meaning CROMWELL, who, it seems, had a design of setting up "a council for the Protestant "religion, in opposition to the congregation *de pro-* "*pagandâ fide* at *Rome.*" See the Bishop's own account in his Hist. vol. i. p. 109.

BUT

But to turn from thefe flattering views, my good friend, to the recital of our late converfation; which I proceed to lay before you with the fame exactnefs and punctuality that I did the former. You will fee the reafon why I cannot promife you the fame entertainment from it.

We had no fooner come together, than Sir J. Maynard began with his ufual vivacity. "I have been thinking, my lord, how dexterous a game I have played with you, in this inquiry of ours into the *Englifh* government. What was obvious enough in itfelf, and had indeed been undertaken by many perfons, I mean the vindication of our common liberties as founded in the ancient feudal conftitution, is the part I affumed to myfelf in this debate; and have left it to your lordfhip to reconcile the FACT to the RIGHT: which is not only the

moft

moſt material point of inquiry, but the moſt difficult; and that which the patrons of liberty have either leſs meddled with, or have leſs ſucceeded in explaining. For, to own an unwelcome truth, however ſpecious our claim may be to civil liberty, the adminiſtration of government from the time of HENRY VII's acceſſion to the crown, that is, for two entire centuries, has very little agreed to this ſyſtem. The regal power, throughout this period, has been uniformly exerciſed in ſo high and arbitrary a manner, that we can hardly believe there could be any certain foundation for the people's claim to a limited monarchy. Add to this, that the language of parliaments, the decrees of lawyers, and the doctrines of divines, have generally run in favour of the higheſt exertions of prerogative. So that I cannot but be in ſome pain for the ſucceſs of your undertaking, and am at a loſs to

conjecture

conjecture in what way your lordship will go about to extricate yourself from these difficulties.

BP. BURNET.

I UNDERSTAND, Sir JOHN, that your intention in setting forth the difficulties of this attempt is only, in your polite way, to enhance the merit of it. I must not however assume too much to myself. The way is clear and easy before me. You have conducted us very agreeably through the rough and thorney part of our journey. You have opened the genius of our antient constitution. You have explained the principles on which it was raised. All that remains for me is, only to solve doubts, and rectify appearances; a matter of no great difficulty, when, instead of groping in the dark, we are now got into open daylight, and are treading in the paths of known and authentic history.

MR. SOMERS.

AND yet, my lord, I shall very readily acknowledge, with my lord commissioner, the importance of the service. For, unless appearances be strangely deceitful indeed, there is but too great reason to conclude, from the recent parts of our history, either that there never was a rightful claim in the people to civil liberty, or that they, as well as their princes, had lost all sense of it. I doubt, the most your lordship can make appear, is, that as our kings, from the coming of the TUDOR line, had usurped on the antient privileges of the subject; so the subject, at length, in our days, has, in its turn, usurped on the undisputed and long-acknowledged prerogative of the sovereign. In short, I doubt there is no forming a connected system on these subjects; but that in our country, as well as in others, liberty and prerogative have prevailed and taken the ascendant at different times,

according

according as either was checked or favoured by contingent circumstances.

BP. BURNET.

STILL Mr. SOMERS, I see, is on the desponding side: and with better reason than before; since, if the difficulty be half so great as is pretended, this change of the speaker is little favourable to the removal of it. However I do not despair, whether these surmises of difficulty be real or dissembled to clear up the whole matter to both your satisfactions. The stress of it lies here: That, whereas a mixed and limited government is supposed to have been the antient constitution in this country, the appearances, in fact, for a couple of centuries, have been so repugnant to this notion, that either the supposition must be given up as too hastily formed, or sufficient reasons must be assigned for these contradictory appearances. I embrace the latter part of this alternative without hesitation or reserve; and pretend to lay before you such unanswerable arguments for the cause I have undertaken, as, in better hands, might amount to a perfect vindication of ENGLISH LIBERTY.

I TAKE my rise from the period which my lord commissioner has prescribed to me; that is from the accession of the TUDOR family.

WE have henceforth, indeed, a succession of high despotic princes, who were politic and daring enough to improve every advantage against the people's liberties. And their peculiar characters were well suited to the places in which we find them. Henry VII. was wise and provident; jealous of his authority as well as title; and fruitful in expedients to secure both. His son and successor, who had a spirit of the largest size,

size, and, as one says [*h*], *feared nothing but the falling of the heavens*, was admirably formed to sustain and establish that power, which the other had assumed. And after two short reigns, which afforded the people no opportunity of recovering their lost ground, the crown settled on the head of a princess, who, with the united qualifications of her father and grandfather, surpassed them both in the arts of a winning and gracious popularity. And thus, in the compass of a century, the prerogative was now wound up to a height, that was very flattering to the views and inclinations of the STUART family.

It may be further observed, that the condition of the times was such as wonderfully conspired with the designs and dispositions of these princes.

[*h*] NAT. BACON, in his Disc. part II. p. 125. *Lond.* 1739.

A LONG and bloody war, that had well nigh exhausted the strength and vitals of this country, was, at length, composed by the fortunate successes of *Bosworth-field*. All men were desirous to breathe a little from the rage of civil wars. And the enormous tyranny of the prince, whose death had made way for the exaltation of the earl of RICHMOND, was a sort of foil to the new government, and made the rigours of it appear but moderate when set against the cruelties of the preceding reign.

THE great change that followed, in the deliverance of the nation from papal tyranny, and the suppression of religious houses, was a new pretence for the extension of the royal prerogative; and the people submitted to it with pleasure, as they saw no other way to support and accomplish that important enterprise.

AND

AND, lastly, the regal power, which had gained so immensely by the rejection of the papal dominion, was carried still higher by the great work of reformation; which being conducted by a wise and able princess, was easily improved, on every occasion, to the advantage of the crown.

AND thus, whether we consider the characters of the persons, or the circumstances of the times, every thing concurred to exalt the princes of the house of TUDOR to a height of power and prerogative, which had hitherto been unknown in *England,* and became, in the end, so dangerous to the constitution itself.

BUT you expect me, I suppose, to point to the very examples of usurpation, I have in view, and the means by which it took effect in the hands of these and the succeeding princes.

SIR J. MAYNARD.

WE do indeed expect that from your lordship. For otherwise it will be thought that what you treat as an usurpation, was but the genuine exercise of the regal authority; only favoured by fortunate conjunctures, and, as you say, by great ability in the princes themselves.

MR. SOMERS.

PERHAPS, still more will be expected. For it may not be enough to tell us, what usurpations there were, or even by what means they became successful. It should further appear, methinks, that these usurpations, though they suspended the exercise of the peoples liberties, did not destroy them; did not, at least, annihilate the CONSTITUTION from which those liberties were derived.

BP. BURNET.

ALL this will naturally come in our way, as we go along. And, since you will

will have me ufurp the chair on this occafion, and, like the princes I am fpeaking of, take to myfelf an authority to which I have no right, let me prefume a little on my new dignity; and, in what follows, difcourfe to you, as our manner is, without interruption or reply.

SIR J. MAYNARD.

This, it muft be owned, is carrying the prerogative of the chair to its utmoft height. But, if we fubmit to it in other places, is it reafonable you fhould require us to do fo here? Befides, your lordfhip forgets that I am too old to be a patient hearer. And Mr. Somers too—

MR. SOMERS.

I can engage, in this inftance, for paffive obedience. And my lord, perhaps, does not infift on the full extent of his prerogative. It is fit, however, we attend with reverence, while fuch an advocate is pleading in fuch a caufe.

BP.

BP. BURNET.

I was saying, that all your demands would be satisfied, as I went along in this discourse. It is true, an attentive reader of our history, who considers what is said of the mixed frame of our government, and the struggles that were occasioned by it, is surprised to find that these contentions at once subsided on the accession of the house of TUDOR; and that the tenour of the government thenceforth for many successions is as calm, and the popular influence as small, as in the most absolute and despotic forms. This appearance tempts him to conclude, that the crown had at length redeemed itself from a forced, unconstitutional servitude; and that, far from usurping on the people, it only returned to the exercise of its old and acknowledged rights. For otherwise it will be said, how could the people at once become so insensible, and their representatives in parliament so tame,

tame, as to bear with the moſt imperious of their princes without reluctance; they, who had reſented much ſmaller matters from the gentleſt and the beſt?

But thoſe, who talk in this ſtrain, have not conſidered, that there were ſome circumſtances in the ſtate of things, from the time we are ſpeaking of, that DISABLED the nation from inſiſting, and many more that INDISPOSED them to inſiſt, on their antient and undoubted rights.

I took notice, that the ruinous contentions of the two houſes of York and Lancaster, from which the nation was at laſt delivered by the acceſſion of Henry VII, diſpoſed all men to ſubmit with ſatisfaction to the new government. Such a conjuncture was favourable, of itſelf, to the increaſe of the regal power. But the truth is, there was little danger of any ſuccefsful oppoſition to the crown,

if

if the nation had been ever so ill inclined towards it. The great lords or barons were, in former days, both by the feudal constitution, and by the vast property they had in their hands, the proper and only check on the sovereign. These had been either cut off, or so far weakened at least by the preceding civil wars, that the danger seemed entirely over from that quarter. The politic king was aware of his advantage, and improved it to admiration. One may even affirm, that this was the sole object of his government.

For the greater security, and majesty of his person, he began with the institution of his LIFEGUARD. And having thus set out with enlarging his own train, his next care was to diminish that of his nobles. Hence the law, or rather laws (for as Lord BACON observes, there was scarcely a parliament through his whole reign which passed without an act to that purpose)

purpose) against RETAINERS. And with how jealous a severity he put those laws into execution, is sufficiently known from his treatment of one of his principal friends and servants, the earl of Oxford [*i*].

IT was also with a view to this depression of the nobility, that the court of STAR-CHAMBER was considered so much, and confirmed by act of parliament in his reign: " That which was principally aimed at by it being, as his historian frankly owns, FORCE, and the two chief supports of Force, COMBINATION OF MULTITUDES, and maintainance or HEADSHIP OF GREAT PERSONS."

To put them still lower in the public estimation, he affected to fill the great offices with churchmen only. And it was perhaps, as much to awe the nation

[*i*] The story is told by Lord BACON in his history of this prince.

by

by the terror of his prerogative as to fill his coffers, that he executed the penal laws with so merciless a rigour on the very greatest of his subjects.

STILL further, to prevent the possibility of a return, in any future period, of the patrician power, this politic prince provided with great care for the encouragement of trade, and the distribution of property. Both which ends were effected at once by that famous act, which was made to secure and facilitate the alienation of estates by fine and proclamation.

ALL these measures, we see, were evidently taken by the king to diminish the credit and suppress the influence of his nobles; and of consequence, as he thought, to exalt the power of the crown above control, if not in his own, yet in succeeding ages. And his policy had this effect for some time; though in the end

end it served, beside his expectation, to advance another and more formidable power, at that time little suspected or even thought of, the POWER OF THE PEOPLE [*k*].

THE truth is, HENRY's policy was every way much assisted by the genius of the time. Trade was getting up: and Lollardism had secretly made its way into the hearts of the people. And, though *liberty* was in the end to reap the benefit of each, *prerogative* was the immediate gainer. Commerce, in proportion to its growth, brought on the decline of the feudal, that is, aristocratic power of the barons: and the authority of the church, that other check on the sovereign, was gradually weakened by the prevailing spirit of reformation.

[*k*] He did not consider that maxim of the Lord BACON, "Depression of the nobility may make a king more absolute, but less safe." Works, vol. iii. p. 296.

UNDER these circumstances, HENRY found it no difficulty to depress his great lords; and he did it so effectually, that his son had little else left him to do, but to keep them down in that weak and disabled state, to which his father had reduced them. 'Tis true, both he and his successors went further. They never thought themselves secure enough from the resistance of their old enemies, the barons [*l*]; and so continued, by every method of artifice and rapine, to sink them much lower than even the safety of their own state required. But the effects of this management did not appear till long afterwards. For the present, the crown received a manifest advantage by this conduct.

[*l*] And yet Lord BACON tells us, that when HEN. VIII. came to the crown, "There was no such thing as any great and mighty subject, who might any way eclipse or overshade the imperial power." Works, vol. iii. p. 508.

THERE

THERE was, besides, another circumstance of great moment attending the government of the younger HENRY. He was the first heir of the white and red roses: so that there was now an end of all dispute and disaffection in the people. And they had so long and so violently contended about the title to the crown, that, when that mighty point was once settled, they did not readily apprehend that any other consideration deserved, or could justify, resistance to their sovereign.

WITH these advantages of situation, HENRY VIII brought with him to the throne a spirit of that firm and steady temper as was exactly fitted to break the edge of any rising opposition. Besides the confidence of youth, he was of a nature so elate and imperious, so resolved and fearless [*m*], that no resistance could succeed, hardly

[*m*] "A man, as Mr. BACON characterises him, underneath

hardly any thought of it could be entertained againſt him. The commons, who had hitherto been unuſed to treat with their kings but by the mediation of the great lords, being now puſhed into the preſence, were half diſcountenanced in the eye of majeſty; and durſt ſcarcely look up to the throne, much leſs diſpute the prerogatives with which ſo awful a prince was thought to be inveſted.

AND when the glaring abuſe of his power, as in the exaltation of that great inſtrument of his tyranny, WOLSEY, ſeemed afterwards to provoke the people to ſome more vigorous reſolutions, a ſingular event happened, which not only preſerved his greatneſs, but brought a further increaſe to it. This was the famous rupture with the court of *Rome:* in conſequence of which, the yoke of papal uſurpations, that yoke under which

underneath many paſſions, but above fear." DISC. Part II. p. 120.

our

our kings had groaned for so many ages, was in a moment broken off, and the crown restored to its full and perfect independency.

Nor was this all. The throne did not only stand by itself, as having no longer a dependence on the papal chair. It rose still higher, and was, in effect, erected upon it. For the ecclesiastical jurisdiction was not annihilated, but transferred; and all the powers of the *Roman* pontiff now centered in the king's person. Henceforth then we are to regard him in a more awful point of view; as armed with both swords at once; and, as Nat. Bacon expresses it in his way, as a strange kind of monster, " A king with a pope in his belly [*n*]."

The remainder of his reign shews that he was politic enough to make the best use of what his passions had brought

[*n*] Disc. Part II. p. 125.

on, and thus far accomplished. For though the nation wished, and, without doubt, hoped to go much further, the king's quarrel was rather with the court, than the church of *Rome*. And the high authority in spirituals, which he had gained, enabled him to hold all men, who either feared or desired a further reformation, in the most entire dependence.

In the mean time, the nation rejoiced with great reason at its deliverance from a foreign tyranny: and the lavish distribution of that wealth, which flowed into the king's coffers from the suppressed monasteries, procured a ready submission, from the great and powerful, to the king's domestic tyranny.

In a word, every thing contributed to the advancement of the regal power; and, in that, to the completion of the great designs of Providence. The amazing

ing revolution, which had juſt happened, was, at all events, to be ſupported: and thus, partly by fear, and partly by intereſt, the parliament went along with the king in all his projects; and, beyond the example of former times; was conſtantly obſequious to him, even in the moſt capricious and inconſiſtent meaſures of his government.

AND thus matters, in a good degree, continued till the acceſſion of Queen ELIZABETH. It is true, the weak adminiſtration of a minor king, and a diſputed title at his death, occaſioned ſome diſorders. But the majeſty of the crown itſelf was little impaired by theſe buſtles; and it even acquired freſh glory on the head of our renowned Proteſtant princeſs.

FOR that aſtoniſhing work of reformation, ſo happily entered upon by HENRY, and carried on by his ſon, was after a ſhort interruption (which only ſerved to prove and animate the zeal of good men) brought at length by her to its final eftablifhment. The intolerable abufes and, fhamelefs corruptions of popery were now fo notorious to all the world, and the fpirit of reformation which had been fecretly working fince the days of WICKLIFF, had now fpread itfelf fo generally through the nation, that nothing but an entire renunciation of the doctrine and difcipline of the church of *Rome* could be expected. And, by the happieft providence, the queen was as much obliged by the intereft of her government and the fecurity of her title, as by her own unfhaken principles, to concur with the difpofitions of her fubjects.

THUS, in the end, Proteftantifm prevailed, and obtained a legal and fixed fettlement. But to maintain it, when made, againft the combined powers that threatened its deftruction, the crown on which

which so much depended, was to be held up in all its splendor to the eyes of our own and foreign nations. Hence the height of prerogative in ELIZABETH's days, the submission of parliaments, and, I may almost say, the prostration of the people.

AND when this magnanimous princess, as well by her vast spirit and personal virtues, as the constant successes of her long reign, had derived the highest dignity and authority on the *English* sceptre, it passed into the hands of the elder JAMES; who brought something more with him than a good will, the accession of a great kingdom, and the opinion of deep wisdom, to enable him to wield it.

WHAT followed in his and the succeeding reigns, I need not be at the pains to recount to you. These things are too recent for me to dwell upon; and you, my lord commissioner, do not only

only remember them perfectly, but have yourself acted a great part in moſt of them. Allow me only to ſay, that from this brief hiſtory of the regal authority, and the means by which it arrived at ſo unuſual a greatneſs, it is no wonder that the STUART family were ſomewhat dazzled by the height to which they were raiſed, and that more than half a century was required to correct, if it ever did correct, the high but falſe notions they had entertained of the imperial dignity.

SIR J. MAYNARD.

IF you permit me, at laſt, to break in at the opening which this concluſion of your diſcourſe ſeems to give me; I would ſay, That, on your principles, the houſe of STUART had great reaſon for the high notions you aſcribe to them. For what other concluſion could they make, but that a power, which had domineered for ſo long a time, and that by the full allowance of parliament and people, was,

both

both in fact and right, abfolute and uncontrolable?

BP. BURNET.

It is certain, the STUART family did draw that conclufion. But a great deal too haftily; as may appear from your own obfervation, that the exercife of this extraordinary power was committed, or more properly indulged to them, by the people. This is fo ftrictly true, that from the firft to the laft of the TUDOR line; imperious and defpotic as they were of their own nature, no extraordinary ftretch of power was ventured upon by any of them, but under the countenance and protection of an act of parliament. Hence it was, that the STAR-CHAMBER, though the jurifdiction of this court had the authority of the common law, was confirmed by ftatute; that the proceedings of EMPSON and DUDLEY had the fanction of parliament; that HENRY the VIIIth's fupremacy, and all acts of power dependent upon it, had the fame foundation:

tion: in a word, that every thing, which wore the face of an abſolute authority in the king, was not in virtue of any ſuppoſed inherent prerogative in the crown, but the ſpecial grant of the ſubject. No doubt, this compliance, and particularly if we conſider the lengths to which it was carried, may be brought to prove the obſequious and even abject diſpoſitions of the times; though we allow a great deal, as I think we ſhould, to prudence and good policy. But then the parliaments, by taking care to make every addition to the crown their OWN PROPER ACT, left their kings no pretence to conſider themſelves as abſolute and independent,

MR. SOMERS.

I DOUBT, conſidering the ſlaviſh diſpoſition of the times, that, if the people ſtill poſſeſſed a ſhew of liberty, this advantage was owing to the pure condeſcenſion of the crown, and not to their
own

own policy. A king that could obtain of his parliament to have his proclamations pafs for laws [*o*], might have ventured on this ftep without the concurrence of parliament.

BP. BURNET.

I ACKNOWLEDGE the act you glance at was of an extraordinary kind; and might feem, by implication at leaft, to deliver up the entire legiflative authority into the hands of the fovereign. But there is a wide difference between the crown's ufurping this ftrange power, and the parliament's beftowing it. The cafe was (and nothing could be more fortunate for the nation) that at the time when the people were leaft able to controul their prince, their prince's affairs conftrained him to court his people. For the rejection of the papal power and the reformation of religion were things of that

[*o*] This terrible act is 31 HEN. VIII. c. 8. It was repealed in 1 EDW. VI. c. 12.

high nature, and so full of hazard, that no expedient was to be overlooked, which tended to make the execution of these projects safe or easy. Hence it was, that no steps were taken by the crown but with the consent and approbation of the two houses. And if these were compelled by the circumstances of their situation to favour their prince's interest or caprice by absurd and inconsistent compliances, this benefit at least they drew to themselves, that their power by that means would appear the greater and more unquestionable. For what indeed could display the omnipotency of parliaments more than their being called in to make and unmake the measures of government, and give a sanction, as it were, to contradictions? Of which there cannot be a stronger instance than the changes they made from time to time, as Henry VIII's passions swayed him, in the rule of succession.

Thus

Thus we see that, through the entire reigns of the house of TUDOR, that is, the most despotic and arbitrary of our princes, the forms of liberty were still kept up, and the constitution maintained, even amidst the advantages of all sorts which offered for the destruction of both. The parliament indeed was obsequious, was servile, was directed, if you will; but every proceeding was authorised and confirmed by parliament. The king in the mean time found himself at his ease; perhaps believed himself absolute, and considered his application to parliaments as an act of mere grace and popular condescension. At least, after so long experience of their submission, the elder JAMES certainly thought himself at liberty to entertain this belief of them. But he was the first of our princes that durst avow this belief plainly and openly. He was stimulated, no doubt, to this usurpation of power in *England,* by the memory

memory of his former subjection, or servitude rather, to the imperious church of *Scotland.* But this was not all. Succeeding to so fair a patrimony as that of a mighty kingdom, where little or no opposition had been made for some reigns to the will of the sovereign; to a kingdom too, securely settled in the possession of its favoured religion, which had occasioned all the dangers, and produced all the condescension, of the preceding princes; bringing, besides, with him to the succession, an undisputed title and the additional splendor of another crown; all these advantages meeting in his person at that point of time, he ventured to give way to his natural love of dominion, and told the people to their face, that the pretended rights of their parliaments were but the free gifts and graces of their kings: that every high point of government, that is, every point which he chose to call by that name, was wrapt up in the awful mystery of his prerogative:

gative: and, in a word, that "it was sedition for them to dispute what a king may do in the height of his power [*p*]."

Such, you know, was the language, the public language to his parliaments, of JAMES THE FIRST. But these pretences, which might have been suffered perhaps, or could not have been opposed, under the TUDOR line, were unluckily out of season, and would not pass on a people who knew their own rights, had saved to themselves the exercise of them, and came now at length to feel and understand their importance. For, as I before observed, the principal cause that had lifted the crown so high, was the depression of the barons. The great property which had made them so formidable, was dispersed into other hands. The nobility were therefore too low to give any umbrage to the crown. But

[*p*] Speech to the lords and commons at *Whitehall.* An. 1609.

the

the commons were rifing apace; and in a century had grown to that height, that on the acceffion of the *Scotch* family, the point of time when the new king dreamed of nothing but abfolute fovereignty [*q*], they were now in a condition to affert the public liberty, and, as the event fhewed but too foon, to fnatch the fceptre itfelf out of their king's hands.

However, in that interval of the dormant power of the commons it was, that the prerogative made the largeft fhoots, till in the end it threatened to overfhadow law and liberty. And, though the general reafon is to be fought in the humiliation of the church, the low eftate of the barons, and the unexerted, becaufe as yet unfelt, greatnefs of the commons, the folution will be defective if

[*q*] It was faid well of this king—" That he fpake peace abroad, and fung lullaby at home: yet, like a dead calm in a hot fpring, treafured up in ftore fad diftempers againft a back-winter." Nat. Bacon.

we stop here. For the regal authority, so limited by the antient constitution, and by the continued use of parliaments, could never in this short space have advanced itself beyond all bounds, if other reasons had not co-operated with the state of the people; if some more powerful and special causes had not conspired to throw round the person of the sovereign those rays of sacred opinion, which are the real strength as well as gilding of a crown.

Of these I have occasionally mentioned several; such as " the personal character and virtues of the princes themselves the high adventurous designs in which they were engaged; the interest, the people found or promised to themselves in supporting their power; the constant successes of their administration; and the unremitting spirit and vigour with which it was carried on and maintained." All these considerations could not but dispose

pose the people to look up with reverence to a crown, which presented nothing to their view but what was fitted to take their admiration, or imprint esteem. Yet all these had failed of procuring to majesty that profound submission which was paid to it, or of elevating the prince to that high conceit of independency which so thoroughly possessed the imagination of King JAMES, if an event of a very singular nature, and big with important consequences, had not given the proper occasion to both.

SIR J. MAYNARD.

I UNDERSTAND you to mean the overthrow of the papal dominion, which had so long eclipsed the majesty of our kings; and held them in a state of vassalage, not only to the triple crown, but, which was more disgraceful, to the mitre of their own subjects.

BP.

BP. BURNET.

Rather understand me to mean, what was indeed the consequence of that event, THE TRANSLATION OF THE POPE'S SUPREMACY TO THE KING. This, as I take it, was the circumstance of all others which most favoured the sudden growth of the imperial power in this nation. And, because I do not remember to have seen it enlarged upon as it deserves, give me leave to open to you, somewhat copiously, the nature of this newly-acquired headship, and the numerous advantages which the prerogative received from it.

The papal supremacy, as it had been claimed and exercised in this kingdom, was a power of the highest nature. It controlled every rank and order in the state, and, in effect, laid the prince and people together at the mercy of the *Roman* pontif. There is no need to recount the feveral branches of this ufurped authority. It is enough to fay, that it was tranfcendant in all refpects that could in any fenfe be taken to concern religion. And who, that has looked into the papal ftory, needs be told that, by a latitude of interpretation, every thing was conftrued to be a religious concern, by which the pope's power or intereft could be affected?

UNDER the acknowledgment then of this fuper-eminent dominion, no fteps could poffibly be taken towards the reformation of religion, or even the affertion of the juft rights and privileges of the crown. But the people were grown to have as great a zeal for the former of thefe confiderations, as the king for the latter. And in this juncture it was, that HENRY, in a fudden heat, threw off the fupremacy; which the parliament, to prevent its return to the pope, very readily invefted in the king.

THERE

THERE was something so daring, and, according to the prejudices of that time, so presumptuous and even prophane, in this attempt to transfer the spiritual headship to a secular power, that the pope himself little apprehended, and nothing but the king's dauntless temper could have assured, the success of it. The repugnancy which the parliament themselves found in their own notions betwixt the exercise of the spiritual and temporal power, was the reason perhaps for inserting in the act of supremacy those qualifying clauses, we find in it [r].

MR. SOMERS.

IT is possible, as you say, that the parliament might be at a loss to adjust in their own minds the precise bounds of

---

[r] Meaning such clauses as these—*as by any spiritual or ecclesiastical power or authority may* LAWFULLY *be exercised*, and, *provided that nothing be done contrary to the* LAWS *of this realm.*

the spiritual jurisdiction, as united to the civil, in the king's person. Yet, in virtue of these clauses, the regal supremacy was, in fact, restrained and limited by act of parliament: and the import of them was clearly to assert the independency of the crown on any foreign judicature, and not to confer it in the extent in which it was claimed and exercised by the see of *Rome*.

BP. BURNET.

IT is true, that no more was expressed, or perhaps intended, in this act. But the question is, how the matter was understood by the people at large, and in particular by the king himself and his flatterers. Now it seems to me that this transfer of the supremacy, would be taken for a solemn acknowledgment, not only of the antient encroachments and usurpations of the papacy, but of the king's right to succeed to all the powers of it. And I conclude this from the nature of the thing itself, from the current

notions

notions of the time, and from the sequel of the king's government.

If we attend to the nature of the complaints which the kingdom was perpetually making, in the days of popery, of the *Roman* usurpations, we shall find that they did not so much respect these usurpations themselves, as the person claiming and enjoying them. The grievance was, that appeals should be made to *Rome*; that provisions should come from thence; in a word, that all causes should be carried to a foreign tribunal, and that such powers should be exercised over the subjects of this realm by a foreign jurisdiction. The complaint was, that the pope exercised these powers; and not that the powers themselves were exercised. So, on the abolition of this supremacy, the act that placed it in the person of the king, would naturally be taken to transfer upon him all the privileges and preeminencies, which had formerly belonged to it. And thus, though the act was so properly drawn as to make a difference in the two cases, yet the people at large, and much more the king himself, would infer from the concession, " that the pope had usurped his powers on the crown;" that therefore the crown had now a right to those powers. And the circumstance of this translation's passing by act of parliament, does not alter the matter much, with regard to the king's notion of it. For in that time of danger, and for the greater security of his new power, he would chuse to have that ratified and confirmed by statute, which he firmly believed inherent in his person and dignity.

Then, to see how far the current opinions of that time were favourable to the extension of the regal authority, on this alliance with the papal, we are to reflect, that, however odious the administration of the pope's supremacy was become,

come, most men had very high notions of the plenitude of his power, and the sacredness of his person. "CHRIST's vicar upon earth" was an awful title, and had sunk deep into the astonished minds of the people. And though HENRY's pretensions went no further than to assume that vicarial authority within his own kingdom, yet this limitation would not hinder them from conceiving of him, much in the same way as of the pope himself. They perhaps, had seen no difference, but for his want of the pope's *sacerdotal* capacity. Yet even this defect was, in some measure [s], made up to him by his *regal*. So that between the majesty of the kingly character, and the consecration of his person by this mysterious endowment of the spiritual,

[s] The bishop does well to say—*in some measure*. For, according to popish prejudices, the sacerdotal character is vastly above the regal. See POLE's address to HEN. VIII. l. 1. where this high point is discussed at large.

it

it is easy to see how well prepared the minds of men were, to allow him the exercise of any authority to which he pretended.

AND to what degree this spiritual character of head of the church operated in the minds of the people, we may understand from the language of men in still later times, and even from the articles of our church, where the prerogative of the crown is said to be that which GOD-LY KINGS have always exercised: intimating that this plenitude of power was inherent in the king, on account of that *spiritual and religious* character, with which, as head of the church, he was necessarily invested. The illusion, as gross as we may now think it, was but the same as that which blinded the eyes of the greatest and wisest people in the old world. For was it not just in the same manner, that by the policy of the *Roman* emperors in assuming the office of *pontifex*

tifex maximus, that is, incorporating the religious with their civil character, not only their authority became the more awful, but their *persons* sacred?

We see then, as I said, how conveniently the minds of men were prepared to acquiesce in Henry's usurped prerogative. And it is well known that this prince was not of a temper to balk their expectations. The sequel of his reign shews that he took himself to be invested with the whole ecclesiastical power, legislative as well as executive; nay, that he was willing to extend his acknowledged right of supremacy even to the antient papal infallibility, as appears from his sovereign decisions in all matters of faith and doctrine. It is true the parliament was ready enough to go before, or at least to follow, the head of the church in all these decisions. But the reason is obvious. And I need not repeat to you
in

in what light the king regarded their compliance with him.

MR. SOMERS.

It is very likely, for thefe reafons, that the king would draw to himfelf much authority and reverence, at leaft, from his new title of fupremacy. But it does not, I think, appear that the fupremacy had all that effect on the people's rights and the antient conftitution, which your lordſhip's argument requires you to afcribe to it.

BP. BURNET.

I brought thefe general confiderations only to ſhew the reverend opinion which of courfe would be entertained of this mixt perfon, THE SUPREME HEAD OF THE CHURCH, compounded of a king and a pope; and how natural a foundation it was for the fuperſtructure of defpotic power in all its branches. But I now haften to the particulars which de-
monſtrate

monstrate that this use was actually made of that title.

And, first, let me observe, that it gave birth to that great and formidable court of the HIGH-COMMISSION; which brought so mighty an accession of power to the crown, that, as experience afterwards shewed, no security could be had for the people's liberties, till it was totally abolished. The necessity of the times was a good plea for the first institution of so dangerous a tribunal. The restless endeavours of papists and puritans against the ecclesiastical establishment gave a colour for the continuance of it. But, as all matters that regarded religion or conscience were subjected to its sole cognizance and inspection, it was presently seen how wide an entrance it gave to the most tyrannical usurpations.

It was, further, natural that the king's power in civil causes should keep pace with

with his authority in spiritual. And, fortunately for the advancement of his prerogative, there was already erected within the kingdom another court of the like dangerous nature, of antient date, and venerable estimation, under the name of the court of STAR-CHAMBER; which brought every thing under the direction of the crown that could not so properly be determined in the high-commission. These were the two arms of absolute dominion; which, at different times, and under different pretences, were stretched forth to the oppression of every man that presumed to oppose himself to the royal will or pleasure. The starchamber had been kept, in former times, within some tolerable bounds; but the high and arbitrary proceedings of the other court, which were found convenient for the further purpose of reformation, and were therefore constantly exercised, and as constantly connived at by the parliament, gave an easy pretence for advancing

vancing the star-chamber's jurisdiction so far, that in the end its tyranny was equally intolerable as that of the high-commission.

Thus the king's authority in all cases, spiritual and temporal, was fully established, and in the highest sense of which the words are capable. Our kings themselves so understood it; and when afterwards their parliaments shewed a disposition to interfere in any thing relating either to church or state, they were presently reprimanded; and sternly required not to meddle with what concerned their prerogative royal and their high points of government. Instances of this sort were very frequent in Elizabeth's reign, when the commons were getting up, and the spirit of liberty began to exert itself in that assembly. The meaning of all this mysterious language was, that the royal pleasure was subject to no control, but was to be left to take its

its free course under the sanction of these two supreme courts, to which the cognizance of all great matters was committed.

This, one would think, were sufficient to satisfy the ambition of our kings. But they went further, and still under the wing of their beloved supremacy.

The parliament were not so tame, or the king's grace did not require it of them, to divest themselves entirely, though it was much checked and restrained by these courts, of their legislative capacity. But the crown found a way to ease itself of this curb, if at any time it should prove troublesome to it. This was by means of the DISPENSING POWER; which, in effect, vacated all laws at once, further than it pleased the king to countenance and allow them. And for so enormous a stretch of power (which, being rarely exercised, was the less minded) there was a ready pretence

from

from the papal privileges and pre-eminencies to which the crown had succeeded. For this moſt invidious of all the claims of prerogative had been indiſputable in the church; and it had been nibbled at by ſome of our kings, in former times, from the contagious authority of the pope's example, even without the pretence which the ſupremacy in ſpirituals now gave for it.

The exerciſe of this power, in the popes themſelves, was thought ſo monſtrous, that MATTHEW PARIS honeſtly complains of it in his time, as *extinguiſhing all juſtice*—EXTINGUIT OMNEM JUSTICIAM [*t*]. And on another occaſion, I remember, he goes ſo far, in a ſpirit of prophecy, almoſt, as to tell us the ill uſe that hereafter kings themſelves might be tempted to make of it [*u*]. His prediction was verified very ſoon:

[*t*] Hist. Ang. p. 694.
[*u*] Something to this purpoſe occurs in p. 706.

for HENRY III learned this lesson of tyranny, and put it in practice. On which occasion one of his upright judges could not help exclaiming, CIVILIS CURIA EXEMPLO ECCLESIASTICÆ CONQUINATUR [x]. And afterwards, we know, HENRY VII claimed and exercised this dispensing power in the case of sheriffs, contrary to act of parliament [y]. It was early indeed in his reign, and when

[x] The name of this reverend judge was ROGER DE THURKEBY. A cause was trying before him in *Westminster-hall*, when one of the parties produced the king's letters patent with a *non-obstante* in it. "Quod cum comperisset, says the historian, ab alto ducens suspiria, de prædictæ adjectionis appositione, dixit; Heu, heu, hos ut quid dies expectavimus? ecce jam civilis curia exemplo ecclesiasticæ conquinatur, et a sulphureo fonte rivulus intoxicatur." p. 784. HEN. III.

[y] Many statutes, and especially 23 HEN. VI, had forbidden the continuance of any person in the office of sheriff for more than one year. HENRY VII dispensed with these statutes. And the twelve judges resolved in 2 HEN. VII, that, by a *non-obstante*, a patent for a longer time should be good. —It seems, the good old race of the THURKEBYS was now worn out.

the state of his affairs was thought to give a colour to it.

I MENTION these things to shew, that since the pope's example had been so infectious in former times, it would now be followed very resolutely, when the translation of the very supremacy, from which it had sprung, seemed to justify it. And we have a remarkable instance in ELIZABETH's reign, by which it may appear that this prerogative was publickly and solemnly avowed. For upon some scandal taken by the popish party upon pretence that the book of consecration of bishops was not established by law, the queen made no scruple to declare by her letters-patent, that she had, by her supreme authority, dispensed with all causes or doubts of any imperfection or disability in the persons of the bishops. My learned friend, Dr. STILLINGFLEET, in commenting this case, acknowledges the very truth. "It was customary, says he, he, in the pope's bulls, to put in such kind of claufes; and therefore fhe would omit no power in that cafe to which the pope had pretended [z].

And it is in this difpenfing fpirit that James I, having delivered it for a maxim of ftate, " that the king is above law," goes on to affirm, in one of his favourite works, that general laws, made publickly in parliament, may, upon known refpects to the king, by his authority be mitigated and suspended upon caufes only known to him [a].

We perceive the ground of that claim, which was carried fo high by the princes of the houfe of Stuart, and, as we have juft feen, brought on the ruin of the laft of them. And to how great a degree this prerogative of the difpenfing

[z] See his Works, vol. iii. p. 806.
[a] *The true law of free monarchies,* in the King's Works, p. 203.

power

power had at length poffeffed the minds even of the common lawyers, (partly from fome fcattered examples of it in former times, and partly from reafons of expediency in certain junctures, but principally from the inveteracy of this notion of the papal fupremacy) we had an alarming proof in HALE's cafe, when eleven out of the twelve judges declared for it.

SIR J. MAYNARD.

YOUR lordfhip has indeed fhewn that the poifon of the papal fupremacy began to work very fatally. If this bleffed revolution had not happened, what could have been expected but that the next ftep would be, to fet the crown above all divine as well as human law? And, methinks, after fuch a judgment in *Weftminfter-Hall*, it could not be furprifing if another fet of men had ferved the king, in the office of the pope's janiffaries, and maintained his right of difpenfing with

with the gospel itself [*b*], as well as the statute-book.

MR. SOMERS.

I must needs think, Sir JOHN, you are a little severe, not to say unjust, in this insinuation; for which the churchmen of our days have surely given you no reason. And as for the reverend judges, methinks my lord of *Salisbury* might be allowed to expose their determination, at the same time that he so candidly accounts for it.

BP. BURNET.

I perceive, my lord commissioner, with all his goodness and moderation, is a little apt to surmise the worst of our order. But I will try to reconcile him to it; and it shall be in the way he most likes, by making a frank confession of our infirmities.

[*b*] Alluding to the doctrine of the canonists, who say, *Papa dispensare potest de omnibus præceptis* VETERIS ET NOVI TESTAMENTI. See *bishop* JEWELL's *defence of his apology of the church of England, against* HARDING, p. 313.

FOR

For another source of the regal dominion in latter times, and still springing from out of the rock of supremacy (which followed and succoured the court-prerogative, wherever it went, just as the rock of Moses, the *Rabbins* say, journeyed with the *Jewish* camp, and refreshed it in all its stations) was the opinion taken up and propagated by churchmen, from the earliest æra of the Reformation, concerning the irresistible power of kings, and the PASSIVE OBEDIENCE that is due to it.

SIR J. MAYNARD.

Aye, there it is, I am afraid, that we are principally to look for the origin of the high pretences of our kings to absolute government.

BP. BURNET.

I SHALL dissemble no part of the clergy's blame on this occasion; and
there

there is the less need, if I were ever so tender of their reputation, as their inducements to preach up this doctrine were neither slight in themselves, nor unfriendly to the public interest.

IT cannot be doubted that the churchmen especially, both by interest and principle, would be closely connected with the new head of the church. Their former subjection in spirituals to the papal authority would of itself create a prejudice in favour of it, as now residing in the king's person. And the disposal of bishopricks and other great preferments being now entirely in the crown, they would of course, you will say, be much addicted to his service.

BUT these were not the sole, or even the principal, reasons that induced so wise and so disinterested persons, as our first reformers, to exalt the royal prerogative. They were led into this pernicious practice

tice by the moſt excuſable of all motives, in their ſituation, an immoderate zeal againſt popery.

It is true, a very natural prejudice mixed itſelf with their other reaſonings. "The crown had been declared ſupreme, and to have chief government of all eſtates of this realm, and in all cauſes." And, though this declaration was levelled only againſt the pretenſions of every foreign, and particularly the papal power, yet, the clergy were given to conceive of it as a general propoſition. The reaſon was, that the people, from whom the juſt right of ſupremacy is derived, having, at this junéture, not yet attained the conſideration, which the nobles had loſt, they forwardly concluded, that if the royal eſtate were independent of the pope, it was unqueſtionably ſo of every other power. They could not, on the ſudden, be brought to think ſo reverendly of the poor people, even in their repreſentatives,

presentatives, as to allow that they had any pretension to restrain their sovereign.

SIR J. MAYNARD.

I could swear to the truth of this account. One of the popes, I forget which, is said to have called the deputies of the third estate in *France*, on a certain occasion, NEBULONES EX FÆCE PLEBIS [*c*]. And though that might not be the language of churchmen in *England*, at this time, it was not far, perhaps, from expressing their sentiments. It is certain, they soon taught their princes, who put themselves to school to the hierarchy [*d*], to talk in this strain; as appears from many

[*c*] See this particular taken notice of in K. JAMES's Works, p. 384.

[*d*] One of them, King JAMES, profited so well by this discipline, that as we are told on very competent authority, "He was the most able prince that ever this kingdom had, to JUDGE OF CHURCH-WORK." *Ded. of Bp.* ANDREWS's *sermons to* CHARLES I, *by the bishops* LAUD *and* BUCKERIDGE.

of ELIZABETH's and JAMES's speeches to the commons.

BP. BURNET.

SOMETHING of this sort, I grant you, but not in the degree you put it, might have an influence on the political reasonings of the clergy. But their zeal for reformation was what prevailed with them most, and carried them furthest into these notions. It is something curious to see how this happened.

HENRY's usurpation of the supremacy, as it was called at *Rome*, appeared so prodigious a crime to all good Catholics, that no severities were great enough to inflict upon him for it. Their writers proceeded to strange lengths. Even our cardinal POLE so far forgot the greatness of his quality, and the natural mildness of his temper, as to exceed the bounds of decency, in his invectives against him. And when afterwards, in
right

right of this assumed headship, the crown went so far as to reject the authority of the church as well as court of *Rome*, all the thunders of the Vatican were employed against this invader of the church's prerogative. The pope, in his extreme indignation, threatened to depose EDWARD. He did put this threat in execution against ELIZABETH. Yet, in spite of religious prejudices, this was esteemed so monstrous a stretch of power, and so odious to all Christian princes, that the jesuits thought it expedient, by all means, to soften the appearance of it. One of their contrivances was, by searching into the origin of civil power; which they brought rightly, though for this wicked purpose, from the people. For they concluded, that, if the regal power could be shewn to have no divine right, but to be of human and even popular institution, the liberty, which the pope took in deposing kings, would be less invidious. Thus the jesuits reasoned on

the

the matter. The argument was pushed with great vigour by HARDING and his brethren in ELIZABETH's reign, but afterwards with more learning and address by BELLARMINE, MARIANA, and others [e].

To combat this dangerous position, so prejudicial to the power of kings, and which was meant to justify all attempts of violence on the lives of heretical princes, the Protestant divines went into the other extreme; and, to save the person of their sovereign, preached up the doctrine of DIVINE RIGHT. HOOKER, superior to every prejudice, followed the truth. But the rest of our reforming and reformed divines stuck to the other opinion; which, as appears from the HOMILIES, the INSTITUTION OF A

[e] This notion was started even so early as HENRY's rejection of the supremacy. Cardinal POLE insists strongly on this origin of kingship in his book, *Pro ecclesiasticæ unitatis defensione*, lib. i. p. 74.

CHRISTIAN

CHRISTIAN MAN, and the general stream of writings in thofe days, became the opinion of the church, and was indeed the received Proteftant doctrine.

AND thus unhappily arofe in the church of *England*, that pernicious fyftem of divine indefeafible right of kings: broached indeed by the clergy, but not from thofe corrupt and temporizing views to which it has been imputed. The authority of thofe venerable men, from whom it was derived, gave it a firm and lafting hold on the minds of the clergy: And being thought to receive a countenance from the general terms, in which obedience to the civil magiftrate is ordained in fcripture, it has continued to our days, and may, it is feared, ftill continue, to perplex and miflead the judgments of too many amongft us.

YET it could hardly have kept its ground againft fo much light and evidence

dence as has been thrown at different times on this subject [*f*], but for an unlucky circumstance attending the days of reformation. This was, the growth of puritanism and the republican spirit; which, in order to justify its attack on the legal constitutional rights of the crown, adopted the very same principles with the jesuited party. And under these circumstances it is not to be thought strange that a principle, however true, which was disgraced by coming through such hands, should be generally condemned and execrated. The crown and mitre had reason to look upon both these sorts of men as their mortal enemies. What wonder then they should unite in reprobating the political tenets, on which their common enmity was justified and supported?

[*f*] In the writings, published by political men for twenty years together before the Restoration; in which the great question of the origin of civil government was thoroughly canvassed.

THIS

This I take to be the true account of what the friends of liberty so often object to us, "That the despotism of our later princes has been owing to the slavish doctrines of the clergy." The charge, so far as there is any colour for it, is not denied: and yet I should hope to see it urged against us with less acrimony, if it were once understood on what grounds these doctrines were taken up, and for what purposes they were maintained by the clergy.

MR. SOMERS.

BESIDES the candour of this acknowledgment, the part, which our clergy have lately acted, is, methinks, enough to abate and correct those hard sentiments, which, as you say, have been entertained against them.

SIR J. MAYNARD.

THIS apology seems indeed the best that can be made for them. But when
one

one confiders the baleful tendency of thofe doctrines, which were calculated to enflave the very fouls and confciences of men, and by advancing princes into the rank of gods, to abet and juftify their tyranny, one cannot help feeling a ftrong refentment againft the teachers of them, however they might themfelves be impofed upon by feveral colourable pretences. Your lordfhip knows, I might proceed to further and ftill 'harder reflexions. But I have no pretence to indulge in them at this time, when a bifhop is pleading fo warmly in the caufe of liberty.

BP. BURNET.

THIS tendernefs to your friends, Sir JOHN, is very obliging. But I would willingly engage your candour, in behalf of our order. Let me prefume, for fuch a purpofe, to fecond Mr. SOMERS's obfervation, " That the *Englifh* clergy have " at length atoned, in fome meafure, for " former mifcarriages."

SIR J. MAYNARD.

BY their behaviour in a late critical conjuncture: and yet, to speak my mind frankly, the merit of their services, even on that occasion, is a little equivocal, when one reflects how unwilling they seemed to take the alarm, till they were roused, at length, by their own immediate object, the church's danger?

BP. BURNET.

AND can you wonder that what concerned them most, what they best understood, and was their proper and peculiar charge should engage their principal attention? Besides, they went on principle, and with reason too, in supposing that no flight or partial breaches of law were sufficient to authorize resistance to the magistrate [g]. But when a general attack

---

[g] The bishop declares his opinion to this purpose very fully in several places of the History of his own times. His and his friend Tillotson's representations

tack was made upon it, and the difpenfing power was fet up in defiance of all law, and to the manifeft fubverfion of the conftitution, the clergy were then as forward as any others to fignalize themfelves in the common caufe of liberty.

SIR J. MAYNARD.

THEIR old favourite doctrine of *nonrefiftance* was, I doubt, at the bottom of this cautious proceeding. But it was high time for them to lay it afide, when they faw it employed as the ready way for the introduction of that popery, which, as you fay it was its firft intention to keep out.

BP. BURNET.

IT certainly was.—But, not to purfue this argument any further, let me return to the main point I had in view, which was, " to account for the growth of the " regal power from the influence of the prefentations to the unhappy Lord RUSSELL, no doubt, turned upon this principle.

" tranf-

" transferred fupremacy." There is ftill another inftance behind, which fhews how well our princes underftood the advantage they had gained, and how dextroufly they improved it.

It feems prodigious, at firft fight, that when the yoke of *Rome* was thrown off, the new church, erected in oppofition to it, fhould ftill continue to be governed by the laws of the old. The pretence was, that this was only by way of interim, till a body of ecclefiaftical laws could be formed; and, to cover this pretence the better, fome fteps were, in fact, taken towards the execution of fuch a defign. But the meaning of the crown certainly was, to uphold its darling fupremacy, even on the old footing of the CANON LAWS.

This conclufion feems probable, if one confiders that thofe canons proceeded from an abfolute fpiritual monarch, and had

had a perpetual reference to his dominion; that they were formed upon the very genius, and did acknowledge the authority of the civil laws, the proper issue, as my lord commissioner has shewn us, of civil despotism. Whoever, I say, considers all this, will be inclined to think that the crown contrived this interim from the use the canon law was of to the extension of the prerogative. Accordingly it is certain, that the succeeding monarchs, ELIZABETH, JAMES, and CHARLES, would never suffer us to have a body of ecclesiastical laws, from a sense of this utility in the old ones; and a consciousness, if ever they should submit a body of new laws to the legislature, that the parliament would form them altogether in the genius of a free church and state [b]; and perhaps

---

[b] The bishop gives the same account of this matter in his History of the Reformation, Part I. p. 330.

would be for assuming a share in their darling supremacy itself.

WITH those canon laws, and for the same purpose, as was observed to us, these princes retained a great affection for the interpreters of them, the canon and civil lawyers; till the genius of liberty rising and prevailing, in the end, over all the attempts of civil despotism, both the one and the other fell into gradual desuetude and contempt: and as the canonists were little regarded, so their law is now considered no further than as it is countenanced and supported by the law of *England.*

BUT to see how convenient the doctrine of the canon law was for the maintenance of an absolute supremacy, it needs only be observed to you, that one of these canons is, " That it is not law-
" ful for any man to dispute of the pope's

"pope's power." And to see how exactly our kings were disposed to act upon it, one needs only recollect that immortal apophthegm of the elder JAMES, already taken notice of, "That it is sedition for "the subject to dispute what a king may "do in the height of his power."

AND as the canon laws are the pope's laws, so we are told, on the same supreme authority, that the *English* laws are the king's. For thus on another occasion his majesty expresses himself.—" Although a "just prince" (I believe I repeat his very words) "will not take the life of any "of his subjects without a clear law: yet "the same laws, whereby he taketh "them, are made by himself, or his pre- "decessors; and so the power flows al- "ways from himself."—And again, "Although a good king will frame all "his actions to be according to the law, "yet is he not bound thereto but of his
"good

"good will, and for good example giving
"to his subjects [i]."

THUS decreed that *great school-master of the whole land* (to give his majesty no harder a title than he was pleased to give himself); and it is difficult to say whence his supremacy extracted this golden rule of *free monarchies*, if not from the pope's own code of imperial canons.

THUS it appears what misconceptions arose, and what strange conclusions were drawn, from the king's supremacy in spirituals. One might proceed further

---

[i] TRUE LAW OF FREE MONARCHIES, p. 203.— What is said of the king's being the *great school-master of the land* is taken from the same discourse, p. 204. His words are these—" The people of a
" borough cannot displace their provost—yea, even
" the poor school-master cannot be displaced by his
" scholars—How much less it is lawful upon any
" pretext to control or displace the great provost
" and GREAT SCHOOL-MASTER OF THE WHOLE
" LAND."

in

in contemplation of this subject; but I have wearied you too much already. You will see from these several particulars how it came to pass that the REFORMATION, which was founded on the principles of liberty and supported by them, was yet for some time the cause of strengthening the power of the crown. For though the exercise of private judgment, which was essential to Protestantism, could not but tend to produce right notions of civil libery, as well as of religious faith and discipline, and so in the end was fated to bring about a just form of free government (as after some struggles and commotions, we see, it has happened), yet the translation of supremacy from the pope to the civil magistrate brought with it a mighty accession of authority, which had very sensible effects for several reigns afterwards. The mysterious sacredness and almost divinity which had lodged in the pope's person, was now inshrined

in

in the king's; and it is not wonderful that the people should find their imaginations strongly affected by this notion. And with this general preparation, it followed very naturally, that, in the several ways here recounted, the crown should be difposed and enabled to extend its prerogative, till another change in the government was required to limit and circumscribe it, almost as great as that of the Reformation.

MR. SOMERS.

I HAVE liftened with much pleafure to this deduction which your lordfhip has made from that important circumftance of the crown's fupremacy in fpirituals. I think it throws great light on the fubject under confideration, and accounts in a clear manner for that appearance of defpotifm which the *Englifh* government has worn from the times of reformation. I have only one difficulty remaining with me: but it is fuch an one

one as seems to bear hard on the great hypothesis itself, so learnedly maintained by my lord commissioner in our late conversation, of the original free constitution of the *English* government. For, allowing all you say to be true, does not the very translation of the pope's supremacy to the king, considered in itself demonstrate that we had then, at least, no free constitution at all, to be invaded by the high claims of that prerogative? If we admit the existence of any such, the supremacy of the church should, naturally, I think, have devolved upon the supreme civil power; which with us, according to the present supposition, is in the three estates of the legislature. But this devolution, it seems, was on the king alone; a public acknowledgment, as I take it, that the constitution of the government was at that time conceived to be, in the highest sense of the word, absolutely MONARCHICAL.

BP.

BP. BURNET.

I was not, I confess, aware of this objection to our theory, which is very specious. Yet it may be sufficient, as I suppose, to reply to it, that the work of reformation was carried on and established by the whole legislature; and that the supremacy, in particular, though it of right belonged to the three estates, was by free consent surrendered and given up into the hands of the king. It is certain this power, though talked of as the antient right of the crown, was solemnly invested in it by act of parliament.

SIR J. MAYNARD.

There may be something in this. Yet your lordship, I think, does not carry the matter quite far enough; and, with your leave, I will presume to give another, and perhaps the truer, answer to Mr. Somers's difficulty. The subject is a little a little nice, but I have not thofe fcruples which may reafonably be conceived to reftrain your lordfhip from enlarging upon it.

I REPLY then directly, and without foftening matters, that this irregular tranflation of the fupremacy is no proof that there was not then a FREE CONSTITUTION, with a legitimate power in it, to which the fupremacy belonged. And my reafon, without offence to my lord of *Salifbury*, is this. When the papal authority was abolifhed, and the queftion came into parliament, " who now became the head of the church;" the fearch after him was not carried, where it fhould have been, into the conftitution of the kingdom; but, as it was a matter of religion, they miftook that, which was only an affair of church-difcipline, to be a doctrine of theology; and fo fearched, for a folution of the queftion, in the New Teftament, and Ecclefiaftical Hiftory.

In

In the New Testament, obedience is pressed to the person of Cæsar, because an absolute monarchy was the only government in being: and, for the same reason, when afterwards the empire became Christian, the supremacy, as we know from *ecclesiastical story*, was assumed by the emperor: just as it would have been by the consul and senate, had the republic existed. Hence our Reformers, going altogether by spiritual and ecclesiastical example, and hoping thereby to preserve their credit against the reproaches of *Rome*, which, as your lordship knows, was perpetually charging them with novelties and innovations in both respects, recurred to early antiquity for that rule.

This attention to ecclesiastical example was, I suppose, a consideration of convenience with the wise fathers of our church: the other appeal to the Gospel, might be a matter of conscience with them.

them. And thus by force of one text, ill-underſtood, *render unto* CÆSAR *the things which are* CÆSAR's, they put the ſpiritual ſword into the king's hands; juſt as by another, *he beareth not the ſword in vain* (for I know of no better authority) the temporal ſword had alſo been committed to his care.

MR. SOMERS.

This laſt intimation, I am apprehenſive, would bear a further debate [*k*]. But I acquieſce in your anſwer to my particular queſtion; I mean, unleſs the biſhop of *Saliſbury* warns me againſt ſubmitting to ſo heretical a doctor.

BP. BURNET.

My lord commiſſioner chuſes to let ſlip no opportunity of expoſing what he

---

[*k*] Mr. Somers had reaſon for ſaying this; for the intimation was no leſs than that the power of the *militia* was not in the king. Sir J. Maynard was of this opinion, when the matter was debated in parliament in 1642. See Whitlocke, p. 56.

takes

takes to be an error in ecclesiastical management. Either way, however, I am not displeased to find that his main thesis keeps its ground; and that, even according to his own account of the matter, the nation, when it gave up the supremacy to the king, was in possession of a free and legal constitution.

On the whole, you give me leave then to presume that the considerations, now offered to you, afford a reasonable account of that despotic form under which the *English* government has appeared, from the union of the two roses down to the subversion of the constitution in CHARLES the First's time.

OTHER causes concurred; but the Reformation was the chief prop and pillar of the imperial dignity, while the constitution itself remained the same, or rather was continually gaining strength even by the necessary operation of those

principles

principles on which the Reformation was founded. Religious liberty made way for the entertainment of civil, in all its branches. It could not be otherwife. It difpofed the minds of men to throw off that fluggifhnefs, in which they had flumbered for many ages. A fpirit of inquiry prevailed. Inveterate errors were feen through; and prejudices of all forts fell off, in proportion to the growth of letters, and the progrefs of reafon.

The increafing trade and wealth of the nation concurred with the temper of the times. The circulation of property brought on a natural relaxation of the feudal fyftem. The plan of liberty was extended and enlarged; and the balance of power foon fell into the hands of the people. This appeared very plainly from the influence of parliaments, and the daring attacks of many particular members on the higheft and moft favoured claims of prerogative. Our kings were

were sensible of the alteration: but, instead of prudently giving way to it, they flew into the opposite extreme, and provoked the spirit of the times by the very reluctance they shewed on all occasions to comply with it. Every dormant privilege of the crown, every phantom of prerogative, which had kept the simpler ages in awe, was now very unseasonably conjured up, to terrify all that durst oppose themselves to encroaching royalty. Lawyers and church-men were employed in this service. And in their fierce endeavour to uphold a tottering throne by false supports, they entirely overthrew it. The nation was out of all patience to hear the one decree the empire of the kings of *England* to be absolute and uncontrolable by human law: and the other gave more offence, than they found credit, by pretending that the right of kings to such empire was divine [*l*]. Every artifice indeed of chicane

[*l*] The doctrines of divine right, as propagated by the churchmen of that time in their books and sermons,

chicane and sophistry was called in to the support of these maxims of law and theology.
sermons, are well known.—Those of the lawyers were such as these—It had been alleged on the part of Mr. HAMPDEN, in the great cause of ship-money, "that by a fundamental policy in the creation of the frame of this kingdom, in case the monarch of *England* should be inclined to exact from his subjects at his pleasure, he should be restrained, for that he could have nothing from them, but upon a common consent of parliament." Sir ROBERT BERKELEY, one of the judges of the king's-bench, affirmed—"That the law knows no such king-yoking policy:"—Sir THOMAS TREVOR, one of the barons of the exchequer, "That our king hath as much power and prerogative belonging to him as any prince in Christendom:" The attorney general, Sir JOHN BANKS, "That the king of *England* hath an entire empire; he is an absolute monarch: nothing can be given to an absolute prince! but is inherent in his person." *State Trials*, vol. i. Such was the language of the guardians of the LAW, that temple or sanctuary, as it has been called, whither the subject is to run for shelter and protection. Had not Mr. ST. JOHN then much reason for saying, as he did on that occasion, "We have the fabric of the temple still; but the Gods, the DII TUTELARES, are gone?" There is the more force and propriety in this censure, as it comes from a man who was himself of the profession. And another

theology. But the season for religious and civil liberty to prevail over the impotent attempts of each, was at hand. The near approach of the *divine form* other of the same order, the best and wisest perhaps that frequented the temple of law in those days, proceeds with a just indignation still further—" These men (said Mr. HIDE, in a speech to the lords) have, upon vulgar fears, delivered up the precious forts they were trusted with, almost without assault; and in a tame easy trance of flattery and servitude, lost and forfeited (shamefully forfeited) that reputation, awe, and reverence, which the wisdom, courage, and gravity of their venerable predecessors had contracted and fastened to their places; and have even rendered that study and profession, which in all ages hath been, and I hope now shall be, of honourable estimation, so contemptible and vile, that had not this blessed day come [the day of impeachment of the six judges], all men would have had that quarrel to the law itself, which MARCIUS had to the *Greek* tongue, who thought it a mockery to learn that language, the masters whereof lived in bondage under others."—Thus these eloquent apologists for law and liberty. The conclusion is, that though in the great bodies of churchmen and lawyers, some will always be found to dishonour themselves, there have never been wanting others to do justice to the public, and to assert, maintain, and preserve, the dignity of their respective professions.

created an enthufiafm, which nothing could refift. It fruftrated the generous views even of her firft and fincereft worfhippers. In the career of thofe ecftatic orgies, the unhappy king could not prevent his minifters, firft, and afterwards the conftitution itfelf, from falling a victim to that fury, which, in the end, forced off his own head.

Such was the iffue of this defperate conflict between prerogative and liberty. The wonder was, that this fatal experience fhould not have rectified all miftakes, and have fettled the government on a fure and lafting bafis at the Reftoration. The people were convinced, that nothing more was requifite to their happinefs, than the fecure poffeffion of their ancient legal conftitution. The recalled family were not fo wife. And in their attempts to revive thofe old exploded claims, which had fucceeded fo ill with their predeceffors, they once more

more fell from the throne, and left it to the poſſeſſion of that glorious prince whom the greatly-injured nation has now called to it.

This then will be conſidered by grateful poſterity as the true æra of *Engliſh* liberty. It was interwoven indeed with the very principles of the conſtitution. It was incloſed in the ancient trunk of the feudal law, and was propagated from it [*m*]. But its operation was weak and partial in that ſtate of

[*m*] This appears even from Mr. Hume's own account of the feudal times; incomparably the beſt part of his *Hiſtory of England*. And it is to be preſumed that, if ſo ingenuous a writer had begun his work at the right end, he would have been led, by the evidence of ſo palpable a truth, to expreſs himſelf more favourably, indeed more confiſtently, of the *Engliſh* conſtitution. But having, by ſome odd chance, written the hiſtory of the Stuarts firſt, and afterwards of the Tudors, (in both which he found it for his purpoſe to adopt the notion of a deſpotic independent ſpirit in the *Engliſh* monarchy) he chuſes in the laſt part of his work, which contains the hiſtory of *England from* Julius Cæsar *to* Henry

of its infancy. It acquired fresh force and vigour with age, and has now at length

Henry VII, to abide by his former fancy; on this pretence, that, in the administration of the feudal government, the liberty of the subject was incomplete and partial; often precarious and uncertain: a way, in which the learned historian might prove, that no nation under heaven ever was, or ever will be, possessed of a FREE CONSTITUTION.

By the FREE CONSTITUTION of the *English* monarchy, every advocate of liberty, that understands himself, I suppose, means, that limited plan of policy, by which the supreme legislative power (including in this general term the power of levying money) is lodged, not in the prince singly, but jointly in the prince and people; whether the *popular* part of the constitution be denominated *the king's* or *kingdom's great council*, as it was in the proper feudal times; or *the parliament*, as it came to be called afterwards; or, lastly, *the two houses of parliament*, as the style has now been for several ages.

To tell us, that this constitution has been different at different times, because the regal or popular influence has at different times been more or less predominant, is only playing with a word, and confounding *constitution* with *administration*. According to this way of speaking, we have not only had *three or four**, but possibly three or fourscore, different constitutions. So long as that great distribution of

* Mr. Hume's Hist. vol. v. p. 472. n. ed. 8vo, 1763.

the

length extended its influence to every part of the political system.

HENCEFORWARD, may we not indulge in the expectation that both prince and people will be too wise to violate this glorious constitution: the only one in the

the supreme authority took place (and it has constantly and invariably taken place, whatever other changes there might be, from the *Norman* establishment down to our times) the nation was always enabled, at least *authorized*, to regulate all subordinate, or, if you will, supereminent claims and pretensions. This it effectually did at the *Revolution*, and, by so doing, has not created a *new plan of policy*, but perfected the old one. The great MASTER-WHEEL of the *English* constitution is still the same; only freed from those checks and restraints, by which, under the specious name of *prerogatives*, time and opportunity had taught our kings to obstruct and embarrass its free and regular movements.

On the whole, it is to be lamented that Mr. HUME's too zealous concern for the honour of the house of STUART, operating uniformly through all the volumes of his history, has brought disgrace on a work, which, in the main, is agreeably written, and is indeed the most readable *general* account of the *English* affairs, that has yet been given to the public.

records

records of time, which hath ever attained to the perfection of civil government? All the blessings of freedom which can consist with kingly rule, the people have: all the prerogatives of royalty, which can consist with civil freedom, are indulged to the king. From this just intermixture of the popular and regal forms, planted together in the earliest days, but grown up at length to full maturity, there arises a reasonable hope that the *English* constitution will flourish to the latest ages; and continue, through them all, the boast and glory of our country, and the envy and admiration of the rest of the world.

MR. SOMERS.

How generous in your lordship is this patriot augury of immortality to the *English* constitution! Yet I dare not be so sanguine in my expectations [*n*].
And

[*n*] A great lawyer, however, and one of the ornaments of Mr. SOMERS's own house, is not afraid to indulge in these generous expectations.
In

And Sir JOHN MAYNARD, I suspect, who has seen the madness of kings and people, in their turns, will hardly expect it from me. It may be sufficient that we put up our ardent vows to heaven, for the long continuance of it. Less than this cannot be dispensed with in an honest man. Every blessing of civil policy is secured to us by this new but constitutional settlement. And may our happy country enjoy it, at least as long as they have the sense to value, and the virtue to deserve it.

SIR J. MAYNARD.

When these fail, our wishes, and even prayers themselves, will hardly preserve

---

In a late treatise, in which he explains, with exquisite learning, the genius of the feudal policy, "These principles, says he, are the principles of freedom, of justice, and safety. The *English* constitution is formed upon them. Their reason will subsist, as long as the frame of it shall stand; and being maintained in purity and vigour, will preserve it from the usual mortality of government." *Considerations on the Law of Forfeiture*, 3d ed. Lond. 1748.

us. Vice and folly, as you say, may do much towards defeating the purposes of the best government. What effect these may have, in time, on the *English* liberty, I would not, for the omen's sake, undertake to say. You, my lord, and Mr. SOMERS (who are so much younger men) may be able, hereafter, to conjecture with more certainty of its duration. It is enough for me that I have lived to see my country in possession of it.

The End of the SECOND VOLUME.

www.ingramcontent.com/pod-product-compliance
Lightning Source LLC
Chambersburg PA
CBHW021151230426
43667CB00006B/344